GRASP ONE SKILL FOR SUCCESS AND REACH ITS END

BY

MUJAHID BAKHT

Hardcover: ISBN: 978-1-961299-80-1
Paperback: ISBN: 978-1-961299-81-8
EBook: ISBN: 978-1-961299-82-5

Published by

Atlas Amazon, LLC

United States of America

Copyright © 2023 by Mujahid Bakht

All rights reserved. No part of this book, "Strength Training for women: Building power and grace", may be reproduced, stored in a retrieval system, or transmitted in any form or by any means, electronic, mechanical, photocopying, recording, or otherwise, without the prior written permission of the publisher, except in the case of brief quotations embodied in critical articles or reviews. For permission requests, write to the publisher, addressed "Attention: Permissions Coordinator," at the following address:

Atlas Amazon, LLC.
244 Fifth Avenue, Suite D210
New York, NY 10001 USA

Grasp One Skill for Success and Reach Its End is a compelling book by Mujahid Bakht. This isn't just any run-of-the-mill guide; it's a thought-provoking exploration of how mastering a single skill can profoundly impact your life and career.

So, what's the big idea behind Mujahid Bakht's book? It's all about zeroing in on one thing you're good at or passionate about and then taking it to the next level. We're often told to be well-rounded and have many skills. But Bakht challenges this notion, arguing that true Success and fulfillment come from focusing intensely on one area. It's about becoming so good at something you're the first person people think of in that field.

Now, diving into what this book teaches us, it's a treasure trove of insights and practical advice. Bakht doesn't just tell you to focus on one skill; he shows you how. The book is a step-by-step guide to mastery, from identifying your unique talent or passion to developing it through practice and persistence.

But it's not just about honing your skills in isolation. Bakht emphasizes the importance of sharing your talent with the world. This could mean teaching others, creating a business around your skill, or using it to contribute to your community. There's a strong focus on not only achieving personal success but also making a positive impact on others. One of the most compelling aspects of the book is its emphasis on continuous learning and adaptability. Bakht reminds us that being an expert isn't a one-time achievement in a constantly changing world. It's an ongoing journey of growth, learning, and evolution.

Moreover, Bakht delves into the power of mentorship and networking. He illustrates how connecting with others who share your interests or have more experience can open doors to opportunities you might have yet to encounter.

And in today's digital age, Bakht doesn't overlook the importance of an online presence. He provides practical advice on leveraging social media and other digital platforms to showcase your skills, connect with a global audience, and build a personal brand.

Towards the end, the book encourages readers to think about the legacy they want to leave. Bakht asks you to consider how your skill can have a lasting impact, influencing and inspiring future generations. It's a powerful call to think beyond immediate success and consider the long-term effects of your work and talent.

Grasp One Skill for Success and Reach Its End" by Mujahid Bakhtis a motivating and enlightening read. It's a call to action to find that one thing you excel at and make it your life's work, not just for personal gain but for the greater good. It's about becoming so intertwined with your skill that when people think of it, they think of you. This book isn't just about personal success and creating a meaningful and impactful legacy through your unique talents and abilities.

TABLE OF CONTENTS

ABOUT AUTHOR 11

CHAPTER 1 17

WHY ONE SKILL CAN CHANGE YOUR LIFE 17

   Why learning just one great skill could be your ticket to success 18

   Case study 21

CHAPTER 2 26

FINDING YOUR SUPERPOWER 26

   Fun ways to figure out which skill will make you shine 27

   A simple quiz to help you know what you're naturally good at 31

CHAPTER 3 37

THINK LIKE A PRO FROM THE START 37

   Learn to think in a way that sets you up for winning 38

   Find out how the pros keep going, even when it's tough 42

CHAPTER 4 47

MAPPING YOUR SUCCESS JOURNEY 47

   Learn how to make a clear plan that will take you from beginner to boss..48

   We'll look at what the road to winning looks like 51

CHAPTER 5 ....**56**

YOUR FIRST STEPS TO BEING BRILLIANT **56**

Get smart tips on starting your learning adventure 57

Discover the best places to find help and get going 61

CHAPTER 6 ....**65**

PRACTICE MAKES PERFECT **65**

Cool secrets to practicing your skill so you actually get better 66

Real-life stories about people who nailed it with practice 71

CHAPTER 7 ....**76**

FINDING YOUR YODA **76**

How to find great people who can guide you and speed up your learning 76

Learn to connect with folks who know their stuff and can help you 81

CHAPTER 8 ....**86**

GOOD VIBES GETTING AND USING FEEDBACK **86**

Find out why feedback is your friend and how to use it to grow 88

Easy ways to keep improving by listening to the right advice 91

CHAPTER 9 ....**96**

WHEN PLANS CHANGE STAYING FLEXIBLE..............96

Tips on changing your game plan while keeping sight of your goal 97

Learn how to bounce back and make smart moves when things change 101

CHAPTER 10 106

TOUGHING IT OUT 106

How to keep your cool when things get tricky...................107

We'll talk about ways to stay pumped and focused on your goal 111

CHAPTER 11 115

THINK DIFFERENT, THINK BIG 115

Learn to use your skill in ways no one else has thought of..116

We'll check out how some people used their skills to do cool new things 120

CHAPTER 12 125

SHARE THE MAGIC TEACHING YOUR SKILL 125

Get tips on sharing your skill without a sweat 128

CHAPTER 13 133

SHOW ME THE MONEY MAKING YOUR SKILL PAY 133

Turn your skill into cash with these smart moves 134

Learn to make the most of your skill in the big wide world 137

CHAPTER 14 ....**142**

BE KNOWN FOR WHAT YOU DO BEST **142**

Use the internet to tell the world about your awesome skill 145

CHAPTER 15 ....**149**

LEAVING FOOTPRINTS YOUR SKILL'S LEGACY.....**149**

Be inspired by stories of people who've made a difference with their skills 150

ABOUT AUTHOR

MR. MUJAHID BAKHT

LIFE HISTORY:- Mr. Bakht is a mature, experienced administrator with thirty-seven years of experience as a businessman in international marketing and public relations. Mr. Bakht is an International Real Estate Specialist, and Professional Business and Projects Consultant. He was born in Pakistan and educated in Pakistan and the USA. Presently American Citizen belongs to a business-oriented family—thirty-seven years Resident of New York, USA.

BUSINESS HISTORY:- Mr. Bakht is a Founder and President of Atlas Amazon, LLC., Mr. Bakht is a business developer and multilingual business specialist in the Caribbean, South East Asia, and the Middle East emerging markets Mr. Bakht has served, met, and hosted many "Heads of the Countries" Also, maintain a close relationship with investors of high net worth in the USA.

CAREER:- Mr. Bakht has been engaged with many multinational companies in the field of international real estate investment, communication, technology, diamond, gold, mining, Pre-Feb housing, wind & solar energy, outsourcing management, and project consulting along with business partners & associates worldwide. Mr. Bakht has participated in major national and international conferences including participated in United

Nations (U.N.O.) conferences.

TRAVEL:- Mr. Bakht is well-traveled and has visited many countries worldwide.

MANAGEMENT EXPERIENCE:- Thirty-seven years of diversified experience in project consulting, marketing, and business management. As a Director of Marketing, Director of Public Relations, Director of International Affairs, Executive Vice President, President, CEO, and Chairman of many national & multinational companies, where he served previously. Mr. Bakht hired and trained many professionals as business consultants in international marketing and supervised them. Mr. Bakht is the author and publisher of multiple books.

PERSONAL HISTORY:- Mr. Bakht married in 1992 in New York City, USA. He is a Father of three children, all three were Born raised, and educated in the United States of America.

Dartmouth College, New Hampshire, USA.
St. John University, Queens, New York, USA.
Syracuse University, Upstate New York, USA.

CERTIFICATES; Certificate of Authenticity from Bill

Rodham Clinton, President of the United States, and Hillary Rodham Clinton First Lady, USA. (July 20, 2000);

HONORS MEMBER; Madison Who's Who of Professionals, having demonstrated exemplary achievement and distinguished contributions to the business community, registered at the Library of Congress in Washington D.C. USA. (2007 & 2008)

HONORS MEMBER; Premiere Who's Who International, professional business executive having demonstrated exemplary achievement and distinguished contributions to the International business community, 2008 - 2009.

CERTIFICATE OF ACHIEVEMENT; The Achievement Award was presented to Mr. Bakht by Stephen Fossler for five years of continued growth and customer satisfaction from 1996 to 2001.

CERTIFICATE OF AUTHENTICITY; from Terence R. McAuliffe, Chairman of Democratic National Committee, Tom Dachle, Senate Democratic Leader, Dick Gephardt, House Democratic Leader, USA. (June 16, 2001);

ERTIFICATE OF AUTHENTICITY; from Terence R. McAuliffe, Chairman of Democratic National Committee, USA. (April 16, 2002).

MEETINGS WITH DIGNITARIES AND HEADS OF THE COUNTRIES:

Honorable. Teng-Hui-Lee, President of Taiwan. 1999.

Hon. Leonard Fernandez, President of the Dominican Republic. 1999.

Prince. Ahmed Fahad Al-Turki, (Saudi Arabia). 2000.

Benazir Bhutto, Prime Minister of Pakistan, 2001.

Dr. Keith Mitchell, Prime Minister of Grenada, West Indies. 2003-2004.

Pierre Charles, Prime Minister of Dominica, West Indies, 2003.

Mr. Charles Sovran, Foreign Minister of Dominica, 2003.

Robert H. O. Corbin Leader & Deputy-Prime-Minister (PNC) Guyana 2004.

Hon. P. J. Peterson, Prime Minister of Jamaica. 2004.

Dr. Kenny D. Anthony, Prime Minister of Saint Lucia, West Indies. 2005.

Hon. Owen Arthur, Prime Minister of Barbados, West Indies. 2005.

Michael de la Bastide, "Chief Justice" and President of the Caribbean Islands. 2005.

Mahmood M. Hussain, the Private Office of His Royal Highness. Dr. Sheikh-

Sultan Bin Khalifa Bin Zayed Al Nahyan, Abu-Dhabi, U.A.E. 2005.

Sultan S. Al Mansoori, Saeed & Mohammed Alnaboodah, Dubai, UAE 2005.

Ibrahim A. Gambari, Under-Secretary-General (United Nations) 2006.

Hon. Villasarao Deshmukh, Chief Minister of Maharashtra, India, 2006.

Hon. Ashok Chovan, Minister of Industries, Maharashtra, India, 2006.

Hon. Liu Bowie, Ambassador of China, United Nations, 2006.

Senator Einstein Louison, Ministry of Agriculture, Grenada.

Hon. Mark Isaac, Minister of State, Grenada, West Indies.

Hon. Brenda Hood, Minister for Tourism, Civil Aviation, Culture, Grenada.

Wayne Smith, Mayor, Township of Irvington, New Jersey, USA.

Orlando J. Moreno, Brigadier General & Military Advisor, (UNO) Venezuela.

CHAPTER 1

WHY ONE SKILL CAN CHANGE YOUR LIFE

"Why One Skill Can Transform You" Have you contemplated how learning only one skill well could majorly affect your life? Indeed, that is the thing we will discuss!

We live in a universe of data and opportunities to do various things. Now and then, it feels excessive, and we need the foggiest idea where to begin. Yet, here's something confidential: you can gain proficiency with certain things. One unique skill can help you a great deal—more than all the others. When you find and improve at a specific something, it can open entryways, take care of issues, and lift you any place you go.

This section will share anecdotes about individuals who did that and how it functioned for them. We'll likewise give you a few thoughts on how you can find your unique expertise and make it sparkle. It's not necessary to focus on being excellent at everything; it's tied in with finding the one thing you can be perfect at. We should begin to perceive how one ability can make a huge difference for you.

Why learning just one great skill could be your ticket to success

Have you ever seen someone working and thought, "They are really good at this"? It might be a chef in your favorite restaurant or a car mechanic who just knows what a car needs by listening to it. They make their job look so easy, right? But what you're actually seeing is a skill they've worked on for many years to get really good at.

This isn't merely about being competent in a job. This level of skill can forge careers, spawn opportunities, and unlock doors you didn't even realize existed. This book guides you on how to emulate this, focusing on excelling in one area rather than being average in many.

Why emphasize a single skill? In our everyday lives, we often feel the need to multitask. However, trying to do too much at once can prevent you from becoming truly exceptional in any one area. Consider this: when you need a problem solved, do you seek someone who is moderately good at many things, or an expert in the specific area you need help with?

Building a career should be about doing what you love. For instance, if woodworking is your passion, imagine turning that into your signature skill. You could become the go-to person for unique, handcrafted wooden furniture.

This journey is about more than just earning a living; it's about crafting a life that fills you with excitement every morning. Mastering a skill offers a sense of pride and identity beyond just performing a job well.

The road to mastering a skill is as rewarding as the skill itself. There's a profound satisfaction in looking back at your progress, from the initial awkward attempts to the seamless ease of experience.

Of course, this mastery doesn't happen overnight. It requires dedication and can sometimes be challenging. The most frustrating days often contribute the most to your growth. Every effort you make in the face of challenges brings you closer to your goal.

Choosing the right skill to focus on is personal and varies for everyone. Start by considering what you genuinely enjoy, something that absorbs you completely.

Once you've chosen, begin learning. This doesn't necessarily mean going back to school or spending a lot on classes. Utilize resources like books, videos, websites, and most importantly, people. Seek out experts in your chosen field and learn from them.

As you learn, apply your knowledge practically. Understanding theory is one thing, but practical application is another. Embrace your mistakes as they are vital learning tools.

Beyond learning and practicing, reflect on your progress. Evaluate what works, what doesn't, and how you can improve. This self-reflection is key to evolving from just doing something to truly mastering it.

When you become proficient, share your skills. This isn't just about showcasing your abilities; it's also about gaining feedback, making connections, and opening up new opportunities. You never know who might take notice and what doors it may open.

Your growing skill could lead to new job prospects, entrepreneurial ventures, or finding a community with similar interests. Like a snowball, the opportunities will expand as your skill develops.

Remember the initial passion that motivated you to start. There will be tough times, but recalling your original enthusiasm will help keep you driven.

So, this book is about discovering that one thing you're passionate about, becoming exceptional at it, and exploring the unforeseen paths it can lead you down. It's about the effort, the challenges, the victories, and everything in between. It's about crafting a life as distinctive and remarkable as you are.

It all starts with a single skill.

Case study

In a world that constantly tells us we need to be good at everything, it's easy to overlook the power of excelling at one thing. You've heard about people who seem to have a golden touch in one area, but have you ever wondered how they got there? The truth is, they're not much different from you and me. They started with a simple step: choosing one skill to focus on.

Now, let's get to the heart of this – the real-life stories of individuals who successfully mastered a single skill.

There's this guy named Ben. Ben's journey started in a small town where he fixed bikes in his parents' garage. He wasn't the strongest academically and didn't go to college. Instead, he turned his love for mechanics into his sole focus. Through years of dedication, Ben became the go-to guy for bike repairs in his town, eventually opening his shop. He didn't try to also be the best at marketing or finance; he stuck to what he knew—bikes. And it paid off. His shop grew, and now he imports rare bike parts for other shops, all because he focused on being the best mechanic.

Then there's Maria. She loved baking with her grandmother as a child. As an adult, she worked various jobs, but none brought her joy. So, she turned her passion into her skill. She started baking in her kitchen, taking orders through word of mouth. Over time, Maria's small home bakery became known for the best custom-made cakes in the city. She didn't spend time trying to learn to be a top salesperson or web designer; she just baked, and she did it with all her heart. People came for the quality they couldn't get elsewhere.

What about tech skills? I know someone named Ali whose story is just as inspiring. Ali was fascinated with coding, spending hours learning it after his retail job. He started off knowing nothing about programming, just that he loved the idea of building something out of nothing. Over time, Ali offered to fix friends' websites for free, using each task as a learning opportunity. His break came when a small business took a chance on him, and his work ethic led to more clients. Now, Ali runs a successful web development agency, and it all started with his decision to focus on coding.

We can always remember Sarah. Sarah was always drawing ever since she could hold a pencil. She didn't excel in school and often felt out of place. However, her art became her refuge and, eventually, her expertise. She started sharing her drawings on social media without any expectations. As her skills improved, so did her following. One viral piece later, and she was being commissioned to illustrate for brands and publications. Art was her one skill, and she leaned into it fully, transforming her life.

These stories share a common thread – each person took a skill they were naturally inclined towards and nurtured it into something exceptional. They didn't spread themselves thin over multiple areas; they dug deep into one.

You might be thinking, "What about me?" Start with what you enjoy or what comes naturally to you. It could be anything – organizing, writing, fixing things, making people laugh, listening, drawing, cooking – the list is endless. The key is to focus on that one skill and keep at it.

Here's how it could look: say you're good at organizing. You start small by helping family and friends. As you get better, you could offer your services locally. With time, word spreads because your work speaks for itself. You didn't try to become a marketing guru or a sales expert; you just organized, and you did it better than anyone else. Before you know it, you could be running your own organizing business, all because you decided to be great at one thing.

The truth is success can sometimes mean being the best at a multitude of things. It's about finding one skill you can excel in and letting that guide you. It doesn't matter if it's a common skill or something niche. It's not the skill itself, but how you develop it and what you do with it that counts.

Remember, all the people you read about were once beginners. They faced challenges had doubts, and there were certainly times when things didn't go as planned. But they didn't let that stop them. They kept at it, day in and day out because they understood that mastery takes time and persistence.

You might face setbacks, and that's okay. It's part of the process. Every mistake is a lesson, and every challenge is a chance to grow. Keep learning, keep practicing, and keep moving forward. It won't always be easy, but the stories you just heard prove that it can be worth it.

And don't worry about the pressure to do everything. Our world is noisy, filled with the hustle and bustle of multitasking and the glamour of being a jack-of-all-trades. But sometimes, the real magic happens when you quiet the noise and focus on that one skill you can nurture, grow, and shine with. It becomes your craft, niche, and unique contribution to the world.

In focusing on one skill, you're not limiting yourself. You're giving yourself the space to excel, to become the person people think of when they need what you offer. Whether it's fixing bikes, baking cakes, coding websites, or creating art – your skill can be the one thing that sets you apart.

So, think about what you love to do. Consider what skill you could enjoy refining every day. Then, take a leaf from Ben's, Maria's, Ali's, or Sarah's book and start your journey. Your one skill is your ticket to a life of fulfillment and success. And one day, someone will tell your story, inspiring the next person to follow in your footsteps.

CHAPTER 2

FINDING YOUR SUPERPOWER

Have you ever watched a superhero movie and wished for your own superpower? Well, you might already have one! It's not about extraordinary feats like flying or invisibility but rather a unique talent that comes naturally to you and brings joy. In Chapter 2, we will explore and discover what that talent is for you.

Each of us has a skill we excel at. You may be naturally chatting with people, skilled with your hands, or brilliant at brainstorming ideas. Our unique ability is often hidden in the everyday activities we love so much that we don't even notice it as something special.

Identifying your superpower is simpler than you think. Reflect on the activities that you enjoy and excel in. Recall moments when you were so engrossed in a move that the world around you seemed to disappear—those moments are hints of your hidden talent.

In this chapter, we'll explore strategies to uncover your superpower. We'll learn to pay attention to the talents that friends and family compliment us on and recall when we felt perfect about our abilities. No treasure map is needed for this journey; it's a path to understanding yourself better.

By the end of this chapter, you'll have a clearer insight into your unique talent. You'll discover ways to enhance and use it to achieve beautiful things. This journey is not just about recognizing what you're good at; it's about embracing what you love and making it a central part of your life.

Fun ways to figure out which skill will make you shine

You know how sometimes you're just naturally good at something? Like when you can pick up a guitar and strum a tune after hearing it just once, or when you're the person all your friends come to when they need advice because you get what they're feeling. We all have that one thing that clicks for us, where doing it feels more like playing than working. That's what this chapter is all about – finding that one skill that makes you light up and stands out.

First things first, think about what you enjoy. Not what makes the most money or what others think you should be good at, but what brings a smile to your face just by thinking about it. For some, it's making others laugh. For others, it's organizing a messy room so everything fits just right. Some folks can make a plant grow with just a glance. What makes your heart do a little dance?

Now, once you have an idea, let's talk about some fun ways to see if this is your true calling, your special something that could become more than just a hobby.

One way to figure it out is to jump in and start doing it more. If you might be the next great home chef, start cooking different recipes. Don't just stick to what you know – challenge yourself. Cook meals from different cultures. Try baking if you usually grill. The more you cook, the more you'll understand if this is your real deal.

What about sharing your skills with others? Teach your little cousin to throw a baseball if you think sports might be your thing. If you've got a knack for painting, help your friend paint their room and see how it feels to spread the joy of color. One of the finest ways to develop your expertise and determine whether you have a genuine passion for a subject is to teach it to others.

Keep track of how these experiences make you feel. Do you get excited every time someone asks for your help with it? Do you find yourself thinking about it when you're doing other things? That's a big clue. When you love something that much, it's more than just fun – it might be your superpower.

Another idea is to start a little project. If you're into writing, start a blog or a journal. If music is your thing, try recording some tunes on your phone or computer. Projects are good because they help you see a start and finish. You'll learn a lot by doing a big chunk of something simultaneously.

Remember to take notes. Write down what parts you like and what parts you don't. Maybe you love playing music but hate trying to record it. You may enjoy writing stories but don't like spelling and grammar. Knowing what you don't like is just as important because it helps you focus on what you like.

It's also cool to watch others who are great at what you think might be your skill. If you could be a great builder, watch some folks who are already good at it. See how they work and what they do. Sometimes, seeing someone else do something great can light up that thing inside you that says, "I want to do that, too!"

Remember to chat with people who know you well. Your friends and family might have noticed you're good at something even before you did. They might say, "You've always been great at organizing things," or "You can make friends with anyone." Sometimes, the outside perspective of people who care about you can shine a light on your talents.

And how about mixing it up? Combine your interests. If you like singing and playing guitar, try writing your song. If you're into sports and making videos, make a sports vlog. Mixing skills can create something special that only you can do.

If you're brave, try turning your skill into a small business. Babysit if you're good with kids, sell your artwork if you're creative, or fix people's computers if you're tech-savvy. When you make something your job, even just a small one, you see if you like it enough to do it daily.

Let's remember to have fun with it. This is about finding your shine, so it should feel good. If it feels like a chore, step back and ask yourself why. You may need a break, or it's not the right fit. That's okay. Finding your skill isn't a race; it's a journey.

Ultimately, the skill that will make you shine is what you can't wait to do again. It's the thing that feels like playing, where time flies by, and you're just having fun. It's the skill that, when you do it, people can't help but notice because you're glowing with joy.

So go on, get out there, and start trying things. Play around, experiment, and, most of all, pay attention to what feels good. The world is like a giant buffet, and you get to taste-test everything until you find the dish—I mean, the skill—that you can't get enough of. That's how you find your superpower. That's how you shine.

A simple quiz to help you know what you're naturally good at

We often go about our days completing tasks, solving problems, and making things happen without considering what we're naturally good at. The truth is, each of us has a unique set of talents and strengths, but sometimes these skills remain hidden or underused simply because we're not aware of them. Knowing what you're naturally good at can be a game-changer. It can steer you towards hobbies, jobs, or even whole careers where you'll not only excel but also enjoy every moment.

But how do you figure out these skills? One effective way is through self-reflection, and a quiz can be a fun and insightful tool for this. So, let's embark on this journey of self-discovery with a simple quiz that can help spotlight your natural talents.

Question 1: Think back to when you were a kid. What activity could you spend hours doing without getting bored?

- Drawing or crafting
- Building things, maybe with blocks or legos
- Reading or telling stories

- Playing sports or other physical activities
- Helping others, maybe with their homework or chores

Question 2: When you have free time now, what's your go-to activity?

- Cooking or baking
- Fixing things around the house
- Writing, maybe a journal or stories
- Dancing, jogging, or some other physical activity
- Organizing gatherings or helping friends with their problems

Question 3: What do your friends and family often praise you for?

- Your creativity and imagination
- Your problem-solving skills
- Your way with words
- Your energy and athleticism
- Your ability to listen and give advice

Question 4: When faced with a challenge, how do you typically approach it?

- By brainstorming and coming up with creative solutions
- By breaking it down into smaller problems and tackling each one
- By researching or writing about it
- By diving in headfirst, even if it means learning through trial and error
- By seeking advice and discussing it with others

Question 5: If you could pick up a new hobby today, which of the following would you choose?

- Taking an art class, like pottery or painting
- Joining a DIY or woodworking workshop
- Writing Something, Like a Blog or a Short Story
- Participating in a new sport or trying out a different form of exercise
- Creating a new group to read and talk about books

Tally up your answers.

If you mostly picked the first options, you have a natural flair for creativity. Artistic pursuits are where you'll shine. Whether through visual arts or crafts, there's a world of possibilities waiting for you to express yourself.

If you lean towards the second option, you're a natural problem solver. Your brain is wired to see solutions where others see obstacles. Whether fixing things, building them, or even coding, your logical mind is a true asset.

The third option hints at a strong inclination towards words and communication. Writing, journalism, public speaking, or any avenue to harness the power of words would be ideal for you.

The fourth set of options showcases a physically active and adventurous spirit. Sports, outdoor activities, and anything that gets your heart pumping is your playground.

Lastly, if you mostly chose the fifth option, you're a people person. Your strength lies in understanding, helping, and connecting with others. Roles like counseling, HR, or any path that involves interpersonal skills would be right up your alley.

This quiz is just a starting point. It gives a gentle nudge in the direction where your natural talents might lie. However, the real magic happens when you explore these paths further.

For instance, if you identified as creative, you could start a small project at home. It doesn't have to be big, perhaps just a simple painting or a DIY craft. The aim is to dive deeper into what you love and discover the nuances of your skills.

Similarly, if you're a problem solver, challenge yourself with puzzles or fix something around the house that's been pending for a while. If words are your strength, write a letter to a loved one, start a diary, or even pen down a poem. For those who are more physically inclined, try a new sport or take a dance class. And if connecting with people is where you shine, maybe volunteer at a local community center or spend more time with family and friends, helping and connecting.

No quiz can define you completely. You're a complex, multi-faceted individual with many talents waiting to be discovered. However, such resources have the potential to serve as the catalyst—the initial impetus needed to get things moving. Once you've started this journey of self-discovery, there's no telling where it might lead. Your natural skills, once recognized and honed, can open doors you never even knew existed. So take this quiz, reflect on your answers, but most importantly, act on them. Dive deeper into the realms you feel drawn to and watch as your natural skills flourish and lead you to paths sprinkled with success and satisfaction.

CHAPTER 3

THINK LIKE A PRO FROM THE START

When you're just starting to learn something new, it can feel like a long road ahead. You see the experts, the people who are so good at what they do, and they're in a different world. But guess what? Every pro started as a beginner, just like you. The trick is to start thinking like a pro from the very beginning, and that's what we'll dive into in Chapter 3.

In this chapter, we'll talk about how to get into a pro mindset, even when you're just starting. It's about believing in yourself and acting like someone who's already good at what you do. This doesn't mean you pretend to know everything. It means you're serious about learning and doing your best.

We're going to look at the habits and attitudes that pros have and how you can start using them, too. It's like dressing up for a job interview. You want to show up looking sharp, even if you still need to be the boss. When you think like a pro, you pay attention to the little details, practice a lot, and don't give up when things get tough.

You'll also learn how to set goals like a pro. Pros don't just say, "I want to be the best." They make a plan with steps on how to get there. And they check on their progress to know if they're heading in the right direction.

So, are you ready to start thinking like a pro? Let's jump in and see how changing your mindset can change the game for you. It's all about starting as you mean to go on. If you think like a pro now, you're setting yourself up for a future where you can be one. It's going to be exciting, so let's get going!

Learn to think in a way that sets you up for winning

Learning to think in a way that sets you up for winning is like learning to ride a bike. At first, you might wobble and fall, but with practice and determination, you'll be cruising down the street with the wind in your hair. This is what thinking like a pro from the start is all about. It's about getting on that bike, no matter how many times you've fallen off, and pedaling towards success.

The first thing you need to understand is that pros didn't just wake up one day at the top of their game. They had to start at square one, just like you. The difference is that from early on, they began to shape their thinking and habits towards those of a winner. But what does that look like in simple, everyday terms?

Let's break it down into stories and examples that illustrate this mindset in action, making it more relatable and easier to emulate in your journey toward success.

Imagine a young woman named Maria who loves to bake. She watches all the cooking shows, idolizes celebrity chefs, and dreams of running her bakery. But right now, she's just working in a small local bakery, learning the ropes. Maria starts her journey to thinking like a pro by showing up enthusiastically every day, ready to learn something new. She doesn't just do her assigned tasks; she watches what the head baker does, asks questions, and practices her skills at home. She reads about baking, experiments with recipes, and shares her creations with friends for feedback.

Now, meet James, a guy with a knack for technology. He spends his free time tinkering with computers and gadgets. James could play around with tech for fun, but instead, he thinks like a pro. He starts a blog to share his knowledge, stays curious, and learns about the latest trends. He doesn't just settle for knowing the basics; he challenges himself with complex projects, even when they seem somewhat out of his depth.

What do Maria and James have in common? They both have a pro mindset. They're focused-driven, and even though they're not experts, they don't let that hold them back. They understand that becoming a pro is a process, and they're committed to it.

So, how can you apply this to your own life? Start by setting a clear goal for yourself. What is it that you want to be great at? Could you write it down? It doesn't have to be a big thing; it just has to be something you care about.

Once you have your goal, commit to learning something new about it every day. It could be as simple as reading an article, watching a tutorial, or practicing a skill. This is how you start building the knowledge and experience that sets you apart.

Next, feel free to ask for help or advice. Pros know that they can't do everything alone. They have mentors, take classes, and network with others in their field. Find someone further along in their journey than you are, and see what wisdom they can offer.

And here's a big one: don't let mistakes get you down. Thinking like a pro means seeing mistakes as lessons, not failures. When you mess up, you will take a moment to figure out what went wrong. Then, get back up and try with this new knowledge in mind.

Also, it's important to stay organized and make a plan. Make your massive objective into a series of smaller, more attainable objectives. Give yourself deadlines and try your best to stick to them. Pros aren't just dreamers; they're doers. They make a plan and then work on the plan.

Be patient with yourself, too. Thinking like a pro isn't about overnight success; it's about steady progress. Sometimes, it might feel like you're not moving forward, but if you're learning and growing, you're on the right path.

Another part of thinking like a pro is taking care of yourself. It might not seem related to your goal, but staying healthy, getting enough sleep, and taking breaks when needed are crucial to your success. You can only perform at your best if you're feeling your best.

And remember to celebrate your successes, no matter how small. Did you master a new skill? Did you make a new connection in your field? Did you hit a small milestone on the way to your big goal? Celebrate it! This keeps you motivated and positive.

Finally, always keep the big picture in mind. Where do you want all this hard work to take you? Visualize your success. Imagine how it'll feel to reach your goal. Let that vision drive you forward when the going gets tough.

Thinking like a pro from the start sets a powerful foundation for your journey to success. It shapes your actions and decisions, guiding you to be proactive, persistent, and positive, no matter where you start. The pro mindset isn't about where you are now; it's about where you see yourself going and the steps you're willing to take to get there. It's a mindset of learning, growth, and resilience, which anyone can adopt with the right attitude and effort.

Embrace the pro mindset, apply it to your daily life, and watch how it changes how you approach your goals. Success isn't just for the talented or the lucky; it's for those who think and act like pros, even before they've become one.

Find out how the pros keep going, even when it's tough

At the point when you take a gander at experts, regardless of the field they're in, there is by all accounts an ongoing idea that integrates their encounters: they continue onward, particularly when things get complicated. The central issue is, how would they make it happen? How would they push past the problematic stretches to make progress?

We should investigate the manners in which these professionals figure out how to continue through to the end whenever hard times arise.

Most importantly, experts comprehend that difficulties are essential for the excursion. They realize that each deterrent isn't a barricade but a venturing stone. They utilize these difficulties as learning to open doors, developing from everyone. When confronted with trouble, rather than surrendering, they ask themselves what they can gain from the circumstance and how it can improve them at what they do.

Yet, how precisely do they handle these issues? First off, they keep their eyes on the objective. This implies they have an unmistakable comprehension of what they need to accomplish. It's not just about having a fantasy or a wish. It's tied in with having a dream so distinctive and clear that it feels genuine to them, even before they've accomplished it. This clearness assists them with remaining on track and not getting diverted transitory misfortunes.

Experts likewise know the worth of a solid, emotionally supportive network. They have significant areas of strength for a framework comprised of family, companions, tutors, and friends who are generally there to support them, offer sound counsel, and listen carefully when needed. In some cases, individuals need the help of those near them to continue to go when times are harsh.

Presently, how would they manage disappointment? Indeed, professionals don't see disappointment in how a great many people do. For their purposes, disappointment isn't something contrary to progress; it's essential for progress. They figure out that if they're not bombing sporadically, they likely need to propel themselves harder. Thus, they accept every disappointment, gain from it, and use it to illuminate their subsequent stages.

One more critical component is their capacity to remain restrained and industrious. Experts set up schedules and stick to them, in any event, when not in that frame of mind. They appear daily, accomplish the work, and focus on their art. This discipline gathers speed over the long haul and prompts a leap forward.

Regarding critical thinking, stars have an exceptional methodology. Rather than getting overpowered by the entire issue, they break it into more modest, more sensible parts. Along these lines, they can handle each section in turn, which makes the case manageable but rather more feasible.

The fact that keeps experts going makes flexibility another quality. They're available to change and ready to turn when vital. If one methodology isn't working, they're adequately adaptable to take a stab at a genuinely new thing. This spryness permits them to explore through dubious times without losing themselves.

Professionals likewise put resources into their abilities and information ceaselessly. They're deep-rooted students, continuously hoping to improve and remain refreshed in their field. This obligation to learning guarantees they have the apparatuses and understanding expected to beat impediments.

As far as mentality, experts keep an uplifting perspective. They're confident people who trust what is happening, regardless of how intense, can be convoluted. This doesn't mean they're gullible or disregard reality. It implies they center around what they have some control over and stay confident about the result.

Moreover, they deal with their energy admirably. Experts realize that they can't go max speed constantly. They perceive the significance of rest and recovery and incorporate time into their timetables to re-energize. This assists them with keeping up with their endurance over an extended time.

One of the main things professionals do is commend the little wins en route. Their confidence and drive are supported by their acknowledgment and dedication to their accomplishments. Perceiving these little triumphs advises them that they are pushing ahead, in any event, when progress feels slow.

In conclusion, experts are energetic about what they do. This energy fills their drive and responsibility. It gets them up in the first part of the day and keeps them burning the midnight oil. At the point when you love what you do, continuing through difficult stretches becomes more straightforward.

Fundamentally, what moves the stars along is a blend of transparency, support, gaining from disappointment, discipline, critical thinking, flexibility, nonstop learning, inspiration, energy to the board, commending progress, and enthusiasm. They don't have a mysterious equation or an enchanted wand that makes difficulties vanish. They have a bunch of perspectives and ways of behaving that they practice reliably.

Understanding these methodologies and attitudes is only the initial step. At the point when you begin utilizing them, that is the point at which the enchantment occurs. In this way, ponder your objectives and the difficulties you're confronting. Consider consolidating these expert ways to deal with continuing when challenges emerge from influence. Remember, it's not necessary to focus on being awesome or never confronting troubles; it's about how you answer those challenges and continue to advance toward your yearnings.

CHAPTER 4

MAPPING YOUR SUCCESS JOURNEY

In this chapter, we talk about planning your road to success. Think of it like planning a trip. Before you start any trip, you need to know two things: where you are now and where you want to go. Planning for success is just like that.

We all want to succeed at something. You want to be great at a job, learn a new skill, or even become a champion in a sport. But how do you get there? That's what this chapter will help you figure out. We're not just dreaming about the end goal; we're looking at the steps to reach that goal.

In this chapter, we won't use hard words or complicated ideas. We'll keep it straightforward. We'll talk about how to set goals that you can reach. These goals are like the stops you make on a long drive. They let you know you're going the right way and allow you to see how far you've come.

We'll also talk about what to do when things get tough. Everyone has times when they feel like giving up. When that happens, you need a plan to keep going. If you hit traffic on your trip, you don't give up; you find a new way to go.

And remember, your plan for success is all about you. What works for one person might not work for another. Your plan will be special because it's made just for you.

Learn how to make a clear plan that will take you from beginner to boss

Learning to make a clear plan that transitions you from a beginner to a boss is like learning to play a new song on the guitar. At first, the chords seem foreign, your fingers fumble on the strings, and the melody doesn't sound right. But with practice and a clear set of steps to follow, the song starts to come together. That's what we're going to do with your success plan.

First things first, you've got to start by knowing yourself. This is about more than what you want to be good at and what you like doing. If you don't enjoy the path, the destination might not be as sweet as you think. So, sit down and have a real talk with yourself. What gets you excited? What do you think about when you should be doing other things? This will give you a clue about where your passion lies.

Now, with your interest pinned down, it's time to look at where you stand with it. Are you a complete newbie, or do you have some knowledge? Being honest about your starting point is crucial because this will shape your entire journey. There's no shame in starting from scratch. Every boss was once a beginner.

Next up is the research phase. You've got the internet, libraries, and the world around you. Find out what it takes to become good at what you're interested in. This could mean looking up stories of people who are bosses in your area of interest. What did they do? How did they start? Learning from others can give you a blueprint for your plan.

The research will help you set clear goals. But goals can't be wishy-washy. They need to be as clear as a sunny day. Instead of saying, "I want to be good at computers," say, "I want to learn how to code in Python." See the difference? The second goal tells you exactly what to do.

Now, let's talk about a timeline. Everything good takes time, and you've got to be real about how much time you're willing to put in. Are you going to spend an hour every day learning? Two hours? The time you put in will usually match what you get out of it. But life is busy, and you have other stuff, so make a doable schedule.

It's also super important to think about the tools you'll need. If you're going to learn to code, you'll need a computer. If you want to cook, you'll need a kitchen with some basic supplies. Getting your tools ready is like laying out your workout gear the night before. It makes starting a whole lot easier.

With your tools set, it's time to learn. There are loads of ways to learn these days. You've got books, online courses, videos, and more. Pick what works for you and get started. Remember, no one becomes a boss overnight. It's all about taking in a little bit each day.

As you learn, you've got to practice. Practice is where the real magic happens. It's one thing to read about how to do something and another actually to do it. If you make mistakes, that's great! Mistakes are like free lessons. Please pay attention to them and learn what not to do next time.

While you're at it, keep track of what you're learning and doing. This could be as simple as writing down what you did each day. This record will show you how far you've come and keep you going when things get tough.

Speaking of tough, there will be days when you don't feel like it. You might think you need to make more progress or wonder if it's even worth it. This is when you need to remember why you started. Keep your eye on the prize and push through. These tough days are what separate the beginners from the bosses.

As you get better, start sharing what you're learning. This could mean helping others or just talking about what you've learned. Teaching is a great way to deepen your understanding, and talking about your journey keeps it real.

Eventually, you'll start seeing progress. This is the time to start looking for opportunities to put your new skills to use. Can you volunteer somewhere? Is there a small project you can work on? Use these opportunities to test your skills in the real world.

And while you're making all this progress, remember to look after yourself. Being a boss isn't just about working hard; it's also about working smart. Make sure you're getting enough rest, eating well, and staying healthy. A sharp mind and a strong body are your best tools.

Finally, as you move closer to your goals, consider the next steps. What's the next skill you need to learn? What's the bigger goal? Being a boss means always looking to get better, to learn more, and to push yourself to new heights.

There's yet to be an exact roadmap for success. Everyone's path is different. But with these steps in mind, you can make a clear plan that will take you from being a beginner to being a boss. It will take a lot of work, but nothing worth having ever is. Keep at it, stay patient, and most importantly, believe in yourself. You've got this.

We'll look at what the road to winning looks like

The road to winning is an exciting one, full of lessons, hard work, and that sweet taste of victory at the end. But what does that road look like? Let's walk through it step by step, imagining you're on this path, aiming for that big win in your life.

Imagine you've got a goal in mind. It's something you've wanted for a long time. Now, think about what winning means to you. Is it getting that job you've been dreaming of? Is it starting your own business? Or it's being able to make something with your own hands. Keep that image of winning in your mind; it will be your guiding star.

Your goal is to start your own business. The first step on the road to winning is to get to know the business world. You've got to understand how it works, what people need, and what you will offer. It's like knowing the rules of a game before you start playing. You can't win if you don't know how to play, right?

So, you start learning. You read books about businesses, talk to people who have started their own, and take some classes. This is where you soak up all the information like a sponge. You're building the foundation of your house—the stronger it is, the higher you can build.

Next up, you have to make a plan. This plan is like your roadmap. You write down what you want to achieve and how you will do it. This includes how much money you'll need, your customers, and what you will sell. A good plan is clear and makes sense; it tells you what to do next.

With your plan in your hand, it's time to start gathering the tools you need. If you're opening a bakery, you need an oven, flour, sugar, and everything else that goes into making those delicious treats. If you're starting a service, like a cleaning business, you need cleaning supplies and a way to get around. Getting your tools ready means you're serious about starting.

Once you've got your tools, you start the real work. This is the grind—the daily effort you put into your business. You're up early, you stay up late, and you're always thinking about how to make things better. Some days, it will feel like you need to get somewhere. That's normal. Every winner has felt that way. But they kept going, and so will you.

As you're working away, it's important to talk to people and get the word out. They call it networking, but really, it's just talking. You tell everyone you know about your business. Some will listen, some won't, but the more you talk, the better your chances of finding someone interested.

You'll probably mess up a few times, too. You spend too much on supplies, or you miss an appointment. That's all part of the journey. The key is to learn from these mistakes. They're like guideposts that help you get better.

When you do make a mistake, don't beat yourself up. Instead, ask yourself what you can learn from it. This kind of thinking is what separates winners from everyone else. They don't see mistakes; they see learning opportunities.

As time goes on, you'll start to see small wins. Your first sale, a good review, or even completing a big order on time Celebrate these wins. They're signs you're on the right road.

But while you're celebrating, don't take your eye off the bigger goal. Winning is about the long game. It's about sticking to your plan and adjusting it when needed. It's about keeping that image of success in your mind, even when it gets tough.

Throughout this journey, take care of yourself. It's easy to get caught up in the hustle and forget why you're doing this. Remember to rest, to have fun, and to spend time with people you love. Success isn't just about work; it's about being happy, too.

As you get closer to your goal, you'll feel like a winner. You'll have confidence because you've faced challenges and overcome them. You'll know how to run your business, how to make your customers happy, and how to keep going when things get tough.

Finally, you'll reach that goal. You'll have that winning moment. When you make your first big profit or realize your business is running smoothly, you can start planning your next move.

That winning moment is amazing, but it's not the end. Winning is a cycle. Every time you win, you'll look for the next challenge, the next goal. Because once you've tasted victory, you'll want it again.

The road to winning is made of all these things: learning, planning, working, talking, making mistakes, learning some more, celebrating small wins, and always looking forward. It's a beautiful road, and it's all yours. Keep walking, keep working, and you'll get there, step by step. And when you do, it'll be worth every second.

CHAPTER 5

YOUR FIRST STEPS TO BEING BRILLIANT

Everyone starts somewhere, right? Even the smartest folks didn't wake up one day knowing everything. They had to start with the basics and build up from there. This chapter is all about those first important steps you need to take on your journey to being good at something.

Think of the first time you tried to ride a bike. It was probably wobbly; you might have fallen off a couple of times, and it took a lot of trying before you could ride smoothly. That's how it is with any new thing you're learning. The first steps might be shaky, but they are the most important part because they set you up for all the great stuff that comes later.

In this chapter, we will talk about how to get started. We'll look at simple, straightforward things you can do to kick off your journey. Whether painting, coding, cooking, or anything else, the beginning is all about getting into the groove and finding your flow.

We'll explore how to find the right resources, how to make a little space in your daily routine for practicing, and how to keep your motivation up even when it feels like you're not getting anywhere fast. It's all about taking it step by step, and before you know it, you'll be doing things you never thought you could.

So, let's get your engines started and begin the ride towards brilliance. It's going to be fun, it's going to be challenging, but most of all, it's going to be worth it.

Get smart tips on starting your learning adventure

Starting a learning adventure can feel like stepping onto a path leading into a thick forest. You know something is amazing waiting on the other side, but the way can sometimes be clearer. In this guide, we'll talk about how to take those first steps with confidence and excitement.

Now, let's think about what you want to learn. It could be anything from playing the guitar to speaking a new language or coding computer programs. Have you got it? Good. Keep that in mind as we move forward.

First, you need to figure out where you're starting from. It's like knowing which entrance of the forest you're at. If you're a total beginner, that's perfectly fine. If you've got some skills already, that's great too! Just be honest with yourself about what you know and what you don't.

Once you know where you're starting, it's time to gather some tools. No, not hammers and saws – I'm talking about what you need to learn. If you're learning to play an instrument, that's your tool. For a language, maybe it's an app or a textbook. For coding, it could be a computer program. These are your tools, and they're key to helping you learn.

But tools aren't only a little use if you don't know how to use them, right? This is where a little research comes in handy. Look for videos, books, or a local class where you can learn how to use these tools. See how others are doing it. It's like looking at a map before you start walking. It'll give you a good idea of the direction you need to go.

Now, imagine your learning journey like building a house. You wouldn't start with the roof, would you? No, you'd start by laying a solid foundation. This means getting to grips with the basics. Take your time with these. Understand them. They're going to support everything you do later on.

How much time should you spend learning? Well, that's up to you, but even a little daily can make a big difference. It's like watering a plant – regularly, and you'll see it grow. Set aside a bit of time each day, even if it's just twenty minutes, to practice or study.

Okay, so you're learning and practicing regularly. Great! But what if you get stuck? This happens to everyone. The key is not to give up. Try looking at the problem from a different angle. Suppose you're learning a language and can't remember words. Try using them in a sentence. If you're learning to code and your program won't work, check each part separately. Sometimes, stepping away for a bit can help. Take a walk, clear your head, and come back with fresh eyes.

As you learn, it's really important to check your progress. This isn't about something other than getting it right every time. It's about seeing how far you've come. You can tune through now or talk briefly in that new language. Celebrate those victories! They're signs that you're moving forward.

Let's talk about motivation for a second. Staying motivated can be tough, especially if looking for immediate results. This can help remind you why you started this journey. You may want to play guitar at a friend's wedding or speak the local language on your next holiday. Keep that end goal in mind. It's the light at the end of the tunnel that'll keep you moving forward.

Another tip is to connect with others who are learning the same thing. This could be in person or online. It's good to share experiences, tips, and sometimes even frustrations. Both of you have something to teach the other. It's like walking through the forest together – you can help each other find the way.

And here's something important: learning is about something other than being the best or the fastest. It's about understanding more today than you did yesterday. It's about being better than you were last week. So don't compare yourself to others. Compare yourself to the past. That's the only comparison that matters.

As you go along, you'll find that things click into place. What was once hard will start to feel easier. The path will start to clear, and you'll be able to see further ahead. When that happens, you know you're getting there. You're learning, and you're growing.

Now, I can't promise that this journey will always be easy. There will be times when you'll want to give up. But remember that every step, even the small ones, is a step forward. And each step takes you closer to where you want to be.

Learning something new is an adventure, and like all adventures, it has its ups and downs. But also, like all adventures, the experience is worth every moment. You'll become stronger, smarter, and prouder of what you've achieved.

So please take a deep breath, grab your tools, and let's step onto that path. It's time to start this learning adventure, one step at a time. You've got this!

Discover the best places to find help and get going

Starting something new can be a mix of excitement and nervousness. You're keen to jump in, but you also want to ensure you're headed in the right direction. It's like when you're new in town, and you need to find the best spots – where to eat, where to chill, where to have fun. In learning, knowing where to find help can make your journey smoother and more enjoyable. So, let's take a stroll through the neighborhood of learning and discover the best places to find help and get going.

First, the internet is your global town square – it's buzzing with resources. Whatever you want to learn, there's almost certainly a website, an app, or an online community dedicated to it. If you're learning a new language, websites like Duolingo can be your starting point. For more technical skills, like coding, platforms like Codecademy serve as a hands-on guide. These sites are like the friendly locals who are always ready to give you tips and tricks.

Books, those trusty old friends, haven't lost their charm either. They're like the wise elders of the town, full of knowledge and stories to guide you. Hit the library or the bookstore and look for the 'how-to' section. Books can offer structured learning and in-depth analysis that's hard to find elsewhere. And the best part? You can take them anywhere, from a park bench to your bedside table.

Now, let's talk about the people around you. Friends, family, or maybe someone you met at a café who shares your interest – these folks are like your neighbors. They're close by and can offer real-world advice. I got a buddy who's a whiz at graphic design. Ask them to show you the ropes. Learning through people can often be more engaging and tailored to you.

Another fantastic spot to find help is workshops and classes. These are like the community centers of learning. They provide a well-organized setting for group study. The classroom setting also provides discipline and a schedule, which can be incredibly helpful. And let's not forget the teachers – those dedicated guides who can spot where you're struggling and help you out.

Communities and forums online are like town hall meetings. They're gathering spots for people who are learning just like you. Websites like Reddit or Quora, and even specific forums like Stack Overflow for developers, are great places to ask questions, share your progress, and get feedback. It's a way to learn that's interactive and dynamic because you're part of a living, breathing community.

Videos and tutorials on platforms like YouTube are like the street performers of the town, offering free shows (lessons) on just about any topic you can imagine. Want to fix a leaky faucet? There's a video for that. Want to play the piano? There's a tutorial for it. The visual and auditory elements can make learning easier for many people, and you can pause and replay as many times as you need.

Social media groups can act like local clubs. Facebook groups, LinkedIn communities, or even specific groups on platforms like Discord can be super focused on your area of interest. You can find groups for enthusiasts, professionals, and beginners. It's a way to stay updated on the latest in your field and meet people who are as enthusiastic as you are.

Now, something must be said for old-school, face-to-face learning, too. Local community colleges, vocational schools, or even cafes and bookshops sometimes hold classes and events. It's like the neighborhood BBQ, where you can learn a new recipe firsthand. The hands-on experience and the ability to get immediate feedback can be invaluable.

Remember, learning is a journey, and like any good traveler, you'll need to ask for directions now and then. Be bold and reach out for help. Whether it's asking someone to explain something you don't understand or seeking a mentor to guide you – it's all part of the process.

It's also worth noting that learning isn't a one-way street. As you gather information and skills from others, share your learning and experiences too. Teaching is a powerful way to deepen your understanding. It's like watering the community garden – everyone benefits, including you.

Lastly, pay attention to the power of practice. This is where you take what you've learned from all these places and put it into action. Practice might not make perfect – because, let's face it, nobody's perfect – but it sure makes progress. Whether it's daily writing, coding exercises, language speaking, or any other skill, the act of doing it over and over is what will embed it in your muscle memory.

In this massive town of learning, every alley and corner holds potential helpers and guides. From books and websites to workshops and communities, help is always around—you just have to look for it. Keep your mind open, be curious, and reach out. There's a whole world of knowledge out there waiting for you to grab it. So tie your shoelaces, pack your bag with curiosity and resilience, and step out the door. Your learning adventure awaits, and there's no end to the paths you can choose. Now, off you go—explore, learn, and grow!

CHAPTER 6

PRACTICE MAKES PERFECT

Have you ever watched someone do something so well that they made it look easy? It could be a friend who can cook a fancy meal without even looking at a recipe or someone at the park who can dribble a soccer ball as if glued to their feet. It's cool to see, right? But here's the thing—they weren't born knowing how to do that. They got that good by practicing a lot. This chapter is all about that magic ingredient for getting better at anything: practice.

When you start learning something new, it's normal to not be very good at it at first. You might miss a few notes on the piano or need to remember some words in the language you're learning. That's okay! Everyone starts there. The secret is to keep trying again and again. That's what practice is. You try, make mistakes, learn, and then try again. And each time, you get a little bit better.

In this chapter, we'll talk about why practice is so important. It's like planting a tiny seed and then watering it every day. It takes time and patience, but slowly, it grows into something amazing.

You'll learn how to make the most of your practice time, so it's not just about doing the same thing over and over but doing it in a way that helps you improve. We'll also share some tips on how to stay motivated because sometimes, practicing can feel like a chore.

So, if you're ready to roll up your sleeves and get to work, this chapter is for you. Practice might not make things perfect—because nobody's perfect—but it makes you better. Let's find out how you can practice smartly and turn your "I can't" into "I can't yet," and eventually, "I did it!"

Cool secrets to practicing your skill so you actually get better

When you're on the path to learning something new, you've probably heard the old saying, "Practice makes perfect." Well, let's get something straight right from the start – perfect is a bit of a stretch because, honestly, no one is perfect. But practice does make progress, and that's what we're after—getting better every day. So, let's dive into some cool secrets to practicing your skills so you get better. No fancy language or complicated theories; just straight talk about how to nail your practice sessions.

Find Your Rhythm

Think about your favorite song and how it gets you moving. Practice can have a rhythm, too. You don't have to stick to the same schedule as everyone else. Are you a morning person who loves the quiet of dawn? Or are you a night owl who finds peace when everyone else is asleep? Find your best time to practice when you feel most alert and alive. Make that your practice zone.

Start Small

When you're looking at the mountain you must climb to get good at something, it's easy to feel overwhelmed. But what if you broke that mountain down into little hills? Start with small, manageable chunks of what you want to learn. Want to be a guitar hero? Don't worry about mastering a whole song in one go. Start with one chord, get comfortable with it, and add another.

Repeat But With Style

Repetition is key, but it doesn't have to be boring. Mix it up. If you're learning to write, don't just write essays; try poems, letters, or even a diary entry. Changing how you practice keeps your brain on its toes and can make the whole process a lot more fun.

Focus on the Fun Bits

Yes, practice is serious business, but it should also be fun. If you enjoy yourself, you're more likely to stick with it. Find what you love about your new skill and give that extra time. Love playing the fun riffs on your guitar? Rock out to those more often. When you enjoy it, it doesn't feel like practice at all.

Use What You Learn

Take your new skill out for a spin in the real world. Are you learning a new language? Try ordering your coffee in that language. Coding? Make a small program for yourself. Using what you learn in real-life situations can boost your confidence and show you that your work is worthwhile.

Watch and Learn

Watch people who are good at what you want to do. These days, you've got a ton of videos online showing pros in action. Seeing the end goal can be a great motivator. Plus, you can pick up tips and tricks just by observing how they do it.

Teach Someone Else

You don't have to be an expert to teach someone else what you know. Teaching can help you understand your new skill on a deeper level. It forces you to think about the details and clarify them. And hey, it feels good to help someone else out.

Stay Curious

Ask questions Lots of them. Why does this work? What if I try it that way? Being curious can lead you to understand your skill in a way that just following instructions never will. It makes practice active, not just something you have to do.

Take Breaks

Have you ever tried to keep reading when your eyes are closing? Not much gets in. It's the same with practice. Your brain can only take so much at once. Short, focused practice sessions with breaks in between can be way more effective than a marathon that exhausts you.

Set Real Goals

Having clear, realistic goals can help you stay on track. "I want to be the best" is great, but it's vague. How about "I want to play this song all the way through without a mistake" or "I want to write a program that does this particular thing"? Specific goals can guide your practice sessions and give you a clear sense of achievement.

Don't Fear Mistakes

Mistakes are not the enemy – they're a big neon sign saying, "Hey, look here! This needs some work!" Don't be scared to mess up. Each mistake is a lesson, showing you where to focus your efforts.

Celebrate Wins

Did you go through a practice session without checking your phone? Need help with a tricky part of the song you're learning? Celebrate these little victories. They're signs you're heading in the right direction. Plus, celebrating makes you feel good, and that's what this is all about.

Tweak as You Go

Be flexible. If something isn't working, change it up. If a particular practice method makes you yawn, try a new one. This isn't about following rules; it's about finding what works for you.

Listen to Feedback

If someone's giving you pointers, listen. It might be what you need to hear to get better. Just make sure the feedback is constructive. It should feel like a helping hand, not a pushback down the mountain.

Keep the End in Sight

Remember why you started. Visualize yourself doing the thing you want to do, and do it well. Keeping your goal in mind can be the light at the end of the tunnel when you feel stuck in the middle.

Make It a Habit

Incorporate practice into your daily routine. Practice can become an automatic routine, like brushing your teeth. It doesn't have to be a big chunk of time. Even 15 minutes a day adds up.

Enjoy the Journey

Finally, remember to enjoy the process. There's joy in getting better at something, bit by bit. The journey is where you learn the most about your skills and yourself.

With these secrets in your pocket, practice won't just be about repetition; it will be about growth and enjoyment. So grab your tools—a paintbrush, a guitar, a keyboard, or a pair of running shoes—and start practicing. Bit by bit, day by day, you'll get better, and you'll have a good time doing it. Let's get to it and see how far we can go!

Real-life stories about people who nailed it with practice

Telling you about practice is one thing, but showing you how it works in the real world is another. So, let's get into some real-life stories about regular folks, like you and me, who nailed it with practice. These aren't fairytales or stories about overnight success. These are tales of sweat, time, and the grit that gets you through the grind. We will walk through their journeys – no shortcuts, just hard-earned steps on the path to getting better at what they love to do.

Sarah's Story: The Marathon Runner

Sarah never considered herself an athlete. She was the person who would rather read a book than hit the gym. But one day, she saw a poster for a marathon raising money for a charity she cared deeply about. Sarah put on her old sneakers and went for her first run, spurred on by the cause. It was hard, and she didn't get far before she had to stop, panting and red-faced. But she didn't give up.

Every day, she ran a little further, pushing through the aches. Weeks turned into months, and Sarah's short jogs turned into long runs. She learned about pacing, proper shoes, and how nutrition played a part in her training. On the day of the marathon, she was among the sea of runners, her heart pounding not just from the run but from the journey it took to get there. Crossing the finish line was her triumph, the culmination of countless hours of practice.

Jack's Story: The Guitar Man

Jack's old guitar had been collecting dust in the corner of his room for years. He'd pick it up now and then, strumming aimlessly, but it never sounded right, so he'd put it back down. One summer, he decided it was now or never. He set a goal: to play at his friend's wedding. It was not a full concert, just one song, but to play it well.

He started with the basics, his fingers sore from pressing the strings, his movements awkward and slow. But he kept at it, day after day. He practiced scales, chord progressions, and, finally, the song he wanted to play. He battled the frustration of missed notes and the temptation to skip practice. When the wedding day came, Jack played the song. It wasn't flawless, but it was heartfelt, and the applause he received was for more than just the music – it was for the dedication it took to get there.

Lily's Story: The Language Learner

Lily had always wanted to learn Spanish. She loved how the language sounded, fast and fluid, like a song. She tried apps and textbooks but needed help to stick with them. So, she decided to practice speaking with native speakers. She initially felt silly, stumbling over her words and mixing up verbs. But she pressed on, practicing every day with anyone who would listen.

She started thinking in Spanish, talking to herself in the shower, and narrating her chores. She made mistakes – a lot of them – but with each one, she learned. After a year, she traveled to Spain. It wasn't until she ordered her meals, asked for directions, and chatted with locals that she realized how far she'd come. She was speaking Spanish, really speaking it, and all those conversations, all those mistakes, had built her fluency.

Mike's Story: The Coding Whiz

Mike's first encounter with coding was a mess of confusing symbols and error messages. It felt like trying to read an ancient language with no Rosetta Stone to help. But Mike was determined. He started with simple programs, deconstructing them to understand how they worked. Each bug he encountered was a puzzle to solve.

Night after night, he'd sit with his computer, coding, and debugging, sometimes forgetting the time as he chased the satisfaction of a program running smoothly. His small successes led him to tackle bigger projects. One day, he launched an app that helped people find local recycling centers – a project close to his heart. It wasn't a blockbuster hit, but it made a difference in his community. For Mike, the countless hours of practice weren't just about learning to code; they were about making something that mattered.

Emma's Story: The Baker Extraordinaire

Emma's first loaf of bread was a disaster. It was supposed to be fluffy and soft, but it turned out dense and hard as a rock. Instead of giving up, she turned her kitchen into her experiment lab. She tried different flours, yeasts, and hydration levels. She kneaded dough after dough, her arms growing strong and her technique refined.

The warm, earthy scent of fresh bread marked her weekends. Friends and family became her taste testers, their feedback her guide. Over time, her loaves became beautiful – golden crusts with soft, airy centers. She opened a small bakery, and the line outside her door every morning was a testament to her practice and persistence.

These stories, while different in detail, are woven from the same thread – the belief that practice, consistent and deliberate, is the way to improvement. There are no shortcuts or secret passages, just the steady, onward march of trying, failing, learning, and succeeding. Whether it's running, music, languages, coding, or baking, the principle remains the same. It's about setting a goal, breaking it down into achievable steps, and then, bit by bit, day by day, practicing your way to it.

These people aren't superheroes or prodigies. They're individuals who choose to commit to practice, to embrace the discomfort of not being good at something at first, and to find joy in the gradual journey of getting better. Their stories are a testament to the power of practice, a reminder that it's not about being the best right out of the gate but improving a little each time.

CHAPTER 7

FINDING YOUR YODA

Finding someone who can show you the ropes—someone who's been where you want to go. We all need a guide sometimes, especially when getting good at something.

Now, when you hear 'Yoda,' you probably think of that little green guy from Star Wars, wise and powerful, teaching Luke Skywalker how to be a Jedi. Well, in real life, a Yoda doesn't have to be a wise old creature from a distant galaxy. It's just a term for someone who has experience and knowledge and is willing to pass it on to you. In this chapter, we will learn about how you can find a mentor of your own.

How to find great people who can guide you and speed up your learning

When setting out to learn something new or aiming to get good at a skill, having the right guide can be a game changer. It's like having a compass in the wild or a map in a big city; it makes everything easier and faster. However, the question arises about locating such guides, such mentors, who may point one properly and accelerate one's education. Let's get down to brass tacks and examine this issue practically.

Looking in the Right Places

First things first, you need to know where to look. Mentors can be everywhere if you keep your eyes open. They might be in your community, online, at your job, or even your family. Sometimes, the best mentors are where you least expect them. You could find a mentor at a local club or group focused on your interest, or you could find them by reaching out to professionals on social media platforms like LinkedIn.

Let's say you want to get better at cooking. Chefs and experienced cooks often love talking about food. You could find a cooking class nearby or a local food market where chefs buy ingredients. Start conversations, ask questions, and show your genuine interest. You'd be amazed how a simple conversation can become a learning opportunity.

Making the Connection

Once you've found someone who could be a mentor, the next step is reaching out. This can be tricky because you don't want to appear pushy. The key is to be respectful and show that you value their time. Start by asking for a small amount of their time for a quick chat or coffee. Be clear about what you hope to learn and why you think they're the right person to help.

For example, if you're learning web design and you admire the work of a local web developer, send them an email expressing that admiration and asking if they would be willing to give you some tips. Most people are flattered to be recognized for their expertise and will be open to helping you out.

Being a Good Student

When you've got a mentor willing to help you, it's important to show you're serious. Do the homework. If they suggest you try something, do it. Show up prepared for your meetings with questions and updates on your progress. This not only shows respect for their time, but it also makes the time they spend with you more effective.

Take the web design example. If your mentor suggests learning a particular programming language, return to them with what you've learned. Please talk about the challenges you faced and the steps you took to overcome them. This demonstrates that you are doing more than merely considering their suggestions.

Giving Back

Mentorship is a two-way street. Think about what you can offer in return. You may have a skill your mentor is interested in learning, or you can help them with a project. Sometimes, just being someone who listens and appreciates their guidance is enough.

If your mentor is a retired business person helping you with your startup, you could help them with technology they're unfamiliar with. Or, if they're still working in the industry, you could offer to volunteer your time to help with their projects. It's about building a relationship, not just taking advice.

Staying in Touch

A mentor isn't just for now; they can be a part of your network for a long time. Keep them updated on your progress, even after you've achieved your initial goals. Let them see the fruits of their mentorship and maintain the connection. You never know when you might be able to help each other again.

For instance, after you've launched your web design career, send your mentor a message updating them on your first successful project. It will give them a sense of pride and achievement in helping you get there.

Keeping an Open Mind

Sometimes, a mentor might give you advice that doesn't make sense to you right away. Keep an open mind. They're coming at this with more experience, and they might see things you don't. Listen to what they say, consider it carefully, and try to see things from their perspective.

The unconventional cooking method your chef mentor teaches results in the most flavorful dishes, or the strange-looking code structure your web developer mentor insists on makes your websites run faster.

Mentorship beyond One Person

Remember that you don't have to limit yourself to one mentor. You can have different mentors for different areas of your skill or life. The chef who teaches you about flavor pairings can be a different person who shows you knife skills.

You might also outgrow your mentors as you get better, and that's okay. It's part of the journey. Each mentor serves their purpose for a stage in your life. Be grateful for the role they play, and don't be afraid to seek out new mentors as you need them.

Finding a mentor is about being proactive, respectful, and engaged. Keep your eyes peeled for potential mentors everywhere you go. Reach out and make the connection with an honest request for guidance. Be a proactive and respectful student. Offer value back to your mentor and maintain the relationship. Be open to the advice given, and don't be afraid to have multiple mentors.

The right guidance can accelerate your learning and take you to places you might have yet to reach alone. So go out there, find your Yoda, and may the force of knowledge and experience be with you on your journey to mastering your skills.

Learn to connect with folks who know their stuff and can help you

Finding someone who knows their stuff, who can steer you in the right direction and help you grow, is like finding a gem. These are the folks who have been around, seen it all, and have figured things out the hard way. They're the ones who can help you skip the mistakes and get right to the good part: getting better at what you love to do. Here's how to go about it without all the fluff.

Getting Started on the Hunt for Wisdom

First up, where do you find these wise wizards? It's not like they hang out at the local diner with a sign saying, "I'll teach you." Nope, you've got to do a bit of detective work. Think about what you're into and start there. If you're into coding, there are many online groups where coders hang out. Into painting? Local art classes or workshops can be hotspots for finding seasoned artists.

The trick is to become part of these communities. Join in on discussions, show what you're working on, and ask for feedback. People love to help out when they see someone genuinely trying to learn. It's not about emailing a hundred experts begging for mentorship; it's about being seen, genuine, and connecting naturally.

Reaching Out Without Being Awkward

Okay, so you've found someone who could be your mentor. Now, you need to get their attention without coming on too strong. It's like making a new friend. You wouldn't just go up to someone and say, "Be my friend now!" That's weird, right? Instead, you start with a chat, maybe comment on something they've done that you admire, and then, when it feels right, you can say, "Hey, I'm really trying to get better at this, could you give me some advice?"

Imagine you've found this cool photographer, and you're really into photography. You could start by commenting on their photos and asking a question here and there. Build a little rapport. Then, after a bit, you could send a message like, "Your photos inspire me. I'm trying to learn more about photography. Would you mind if I asked you a few questions about your process?"

Be the Best Protégé

So, you've got someone willing to help you out. What now? You've got to show them you're worth their time. Be ready with questions, put their advice into action, and let them see their efforts are going somewhere. If they give you a book or a website to learn from, you should be looking at it that same night.

Say your new photographer friend suggests a certain technique to improve your shots. Next time you chat, you should be able to talk about what you tried, what worked, and what didn't. They'll see you're serious, and they'll probably be even more willing to help.

Don't Just Take—Give, Too

You might think, "But I'm just learning; what can I give them?" Well, everyone's got something to offer. You may be a whiz with computers, and your mentor's still figuring out how to switch from Internet Explorer to Chrome. Offer to help them out. Or be a sounding board for their ideas. Even a fresh perspective can be a big thank you for their help.

Stay on the Radar

When someone puts time into helping you, could you keep them in the loop? They'll appreciate hearing about your progress. It's rewarding for them to see that their help has contributed to someone else's success. So, after a while, drop them an update. It could be as simple as, "Hey, I just wanted to say thanks again for your advice on those photos. I entered a competition and got an honorable mention!"

Listen Up

Sometimes, what your mentor tells you might need to be clarified. That's okay. They're coming at this from a different angle. They've got experience you don't. Listen, take it in, and try it out before you decide it's not for you. The best insights often come from the most unexpected advice.

Not Just One Guru

You don't have to stick to one person. Spread your wings and learn from different people. Each one will teach you something unique. And sometimes, you outgrow a mentor. That's life. It's not a bad thing; it means you've learned what you can from them, and it's time to move on. Always with respect and gratitude, of course.

Real Talk

Finding a mentor is about building relationships. It's about finding someone who knows more than you in an area you're passionate about and building a genuine connection. It's about showing up, being eager to learn, and giving back however possible. And it's about keeping those connections alive, growing with them, and one day, being that mentor for someone else.

These connections make all the difference. They can open doors for you that you didn't even know existed. They can help you learn faster, dodge common pitfalls, and get to where you want to be much more smoothly. All it takes from you is the courage to reach out, the humility to listen and learn, and the willingness to do the work.

It's these human connections that can give you the richest learning experiences. Machines and books are great, but nothing beats the nuanced wisdom you get from someone who's walked the path you're on. So find your guides, your mentors, the ones who can help you rise. The journey's worth it, and so is the destination.

CHAPTER 8

GOOD VIBES GETTING AND USING FEEDBACK

In this chapter, let's talk about something super important: feedback. Feedback is like getting directions when you need help. It helps you to figure out if you're on the right track and how you can get to where you want to be even faster. In this chapter, we will look at how to get good feedback and what to do with it once you've got it.

Imagine you're learning to cook. You try making spaghetti for the first time. You think it tastes alright, but then someone comes along and tells you, "Hey, this is good, but maybe add a little salt next time." That's feedback. It's not saying your spaghetti is bad; it's just giving you a tip to make it even better.

But getting feedback can be scary. It can feel like you're showing someone your diary. It's personal. You put your time and heart into something, and now someone else will tell you what they think. The trick is to remember that most people want to help you, not make you feel bad.

We'll also talk about who to ask for feedback. You don't want to ask just anyone. Your best buddy might tell you your spaghetti is the best in the world because they don't want to hurt your feelings. But your granny, who's been making spaghetti for 50 years, will give you the real deal on what's working and what's not.

Then, there's the part about using feedback. This can be tough. Sometimes, feedback can be a bummer, especially if you thought you were doing great. But here's the thing: feedback is a gift. Someone is taking the time to help you improve. Even if it stings a little, it's worth listening to.

We'll cover how to tell the difference between useful feedback and stuff that could be more helpful. Because let's be honest, not all feedback is created equal. Some of it can send you in the wrong direction. We'll learn how to say thanks but no thanks to that kind.

In the end, feedback is all about getting better at whatever you're passionate about. It's about learning, growing, and becoming awesome at your work. And that's something worth getting a little uncomfortable for. Let's dive in and learn how to work feedback like a pro.

Find out why feedback is your friend and how to use it to grow

Feedback. Just hearing the word can make some of us cringe. We're back at school, worried about what the teacher will say about our essay. But here's the thing – feedback isn't the enemy. It's one of your best pals on getting better at anything. Over the next bunch of pages, we're going to unpack why feedback is so valuable and how you can use it to give your skills a serious boost.

First off, let's clear the air about what feedback is. It's not just criticism. It's not someone telling you what you did wrong to make you feel bad. No, feedback is someone taking their time to give you pointers that can help you improve. It's like when you're playing a video game, and you keep getting knocked out at the same spot. Then your friend, who's already beaten the game, leans over and says, "Try jumping over that rock instead of running around it." That's feedback – and suddenly, you're past that tricky part, feeling like a champ.

Now, why is feedback so important? Well, think about it. When learning something new, you can't always see what you're doing from the outside. You're in your head, trying to get it right. But someone watching you can see the things you might miss. They can be your extra set of eyes. This outside perspective is gold because it shows you what you can't see by yourself.

How do you go about getting feedback? It's not just about throwing your work out and hoping someone will take a look. You've got to be smart about it. Find people who know their stuff. If you're learning to play the guitar, ask someone who can play well to listen to you strum. If you're trying to write better, ask someone with a way with words to read your stuff.

But it's about more than finding an expert. You want someone who's not only good at what they do but also good at giving feedback. There's an art to it. The best feedback-givers know how to say things in a way that helps you without making you feel like you want to give up. They know how to spot the good stuff in what you're doing and help you see how to make the not-so-good stuff better.

When you've found the right people, it's all about how you ask for their feedback. Be clear about what you want. Do you want them to look at everything you're doing or just one part of it? Do you need advice on the basics, or are you looking to fine-tune the details? The clearer you are, the better the feedback you'll get.

Now, brace yourself. When the feedback comes, it might not all be pats on the back. There might be some tough stuff to hear. That's okay. Remember, it's all about getting better. No one, absolutely no one, starts perfect. Every bit of feedback is a step towards improvement.

And that's where the real magic happens – using the feedback. This part is on you. It's about taking what you've heard and thinking it through. What makes sense? What resonates with you? Then, it's time to roll up your sleeves and get to work. Tweak your techniques, change up your approach, and try again. And then, guess what? You ask for more feedback. It's a loop, but a loop that's spiraling you upwards.

There's one more piece to this feedback puzzle – knowing what to ignore. Not all advice is good, even with the best intentions. Sometimes, feedback can be more about the other person's preferences than helping you improve. Learn to say thanks, sift through it, and stick to what helps you move forward.

Here's another thing – don't wait too long to ask for feedback. You don't need to have everything polished and perfect. That's like waiting until you're clean before you take a shower. Feedback's great when you're just starting, and it's great when you think you're almost done. It's always the right time.

As you get better at receiving feedback, you'll start to notice something cool – you'll begin to self-correct. You'll start to anticipate what someone might say and adjust before you ask them. That's you, growing. That's you, becoming more of a pro at whatever you're doing.

Lastly, remember to give yourself some credit. Every time you ask for feedback, you're stepping out of your comfort zone. That takes guts. Every time you use that feedback to improve, you're putting in the work. That takes dedication. Be proud of yourself for that. It's a big deal.

Remember the fun part. Feedback can be fun. Seriously. It's fun to get better at things. It's fun to see progress. So go ahead, find your people, ask for their thoughts, and then do something great with what they tell you. You've got this. Let's turn that feedback into your stepping stones to something brilliant.

Easy ways to keep improving by listening to the right advice

Improving at anything is a journey. It's like learning to ride a bike or getting better at cooking your favorite dish. It doesn't happen all at once, and there are no shortcuts. But one of the most powerful tools in this journey is learning how to use advice—the good kind that nudges you forward. This is about the easy ways to improve by tuning into the right advice and making it work for you.

First things first, where do you find the right advice? It can come from all sorts of places. From the people who've been in your shoes to the experts who share their knowledge on the internet, the right advice can be just a conversation or a click away. But it's not just about getting advice; it's about getting the right advice that works for you.

Imagine you're trying to get better at basketball. You wouldn't take advice from someone who's never played the game, right? You'd listen to a coach or a player who knows the game inside out. The same goes for anything you're trying to improve. Find people who have been successful in what you want to do and see what they have to say.

Now, having a lot of advice can be overwhelming, like having too many cooks in the kitchen. So, what do you do? You filter. You listen to everything but only keep what makes sense for you. It's like when you're picking out clothes to wear. You know what fits you and what doesn't. Apply the same principle here. Use what fits your situation and your style of learning.

When you've got that advice, the real work begins—putting it into action. Advice without action is like a car without fuel; it won't get you anywhere. Pick one piece of advice and give it a go. If you're trying to write better, and someone suggests reading more to improve your writing, start with one book. Could you pick it up and read a little each day? You're not just reading; you're fueling your writing.

Keep track of what works and what doesn't. It's like when you add spices to your food. Some you'll love, and some you might not. When you try out advice, some of it will make a difference, and some will not. That's okay. The important thing is to notice what's changing things for the better. This is how you get better—bit by bit, piece by piece.

What about when the advice seems solid but takes time to follow? Say you're learning a new language, and the advice is to practice speaking every day. But you're shy or nervous. That's when you need to break it down into smaller steps. You could start by talking to yourself in the mirror. Then, you move on to chatting with a friend. Before you know it, you're having conversations in your new language. Small steps lead to big leaps.

Sometimes, the right advice will come from people who care about you, but it might only be what you want to hear. It's like when a friend tells you you've got something stuck in your teeth. It may be embarrassing, but it's helpful. If the advice is honest and meant to help you, even if it's a bit tough, it's worth listening to.

Remember that advice is a two-way street. Just as you take advice, you can give it, too. Sharing what works for you might help someone else get better. And talking about what you're learning can reinforce it in your mind. It's like explaining how to do something to someone else; you understand it better.

One of the most important things about advice is knowing when to say, "Thanks, but no thanks." Not all advice is good advice for you. If you've tried it and it's not working, it's okay to let it go.

It's like when you try a new food and don't like it. You don't have to keep eating it. Same with advice—take what helps and leave what doesn't.

And don't remember to pat yourself on the back for the progress you're making. Every time you use advice to get a little better, you're winning. You're moving forward. That's what it's all about.

Now, let's not kid ourselves; using advice to improve is not always going to be easy. Sometimes it's going to be hard work. But that's the deal with anything worth doing. The good news is the more you do it, the easier it gets. Each piece of advice you use to improve is like adding a tool to your toolbox. Before you know it, you've got a whole set of tools at your disposal.

And let's remember the digital world we live in. The internet is a goldmine of helpful information and hints. Online forums, video tutorials, articles, and blogs—there's so much out there. Use these resources. Find communities that are interested in the same things as you. Engage with them. Learn from their experiences and share your own.

Lastly, keep an open mind. Be willing to try new things and different approaches. What works for someone else might work for you, too. And sometimes, the most unexpected advice can be the key that unlocks your potential.

Improving at anything takes time and effort. But with the right advice and the willingness to put it into practice, you can make steady progress toward your goals. Every piece of advice you take and use to get better is like a stepping stone on your path to success. Keep stepping, keep learning, and keep getting better. The journey might be long, but every step counts, and the view improves with every new height you reach.

CHAPTER 9

WHEN PLANS CHANGE STAYING FLEXIBLE

Life can be as unpredictable as the weather. One minute, you've got sunshine and clear skies, and the next, you're reaching for an umbrella. This chapter is all about staying flexible—being ready to move and change when your plans don't go the way you thought they would.

Think about when you're planning to meet a friend. You might decide on a time and place, but sometimes stuff comes up. Maybe your friend gets stuck in traffic, or you do. The place you wanted to go may be closed. What do you do? You adjust. You find a new place, or you reschedule. You don't just give up on seeing your friend, right?

That's the kind of flexibility we're talking about here. It's about having a plan but being ready to change it. You still need to stick to your goals. It just means you're smart enough to know that sometimes the path to your goals takes a few unexpected turns.

In this chapter, we will look at how to be okay with change and make it work for you. It's like learning to dance; when the music changes, you change your steps. We'll explore how to keep your eyes on where you want to go, even when you have to take a different route to get there.

So buckle up, and let's get ready to learn how to stay steady, even when the ground is shifting under your feet. It's all about learning to be as flexible as a tree that bends in the wind—that way, you don't break, you sway. And before you know it, you're back on track, sometimes even closer to your goals than you were before.

Tips on changing your game plan while keeping sight of your goal

When you first set out on any new journey, be it learning a new language, starting a business, or even getting in shape, you have a goal in mind. This goal is like the destination you enter into your GPS. You expect to follow the route and get there without any hitches. But, as anyone who's ever taken a road trip knows, it can be more complicated. There are detours and roadblocks, and sometimes, the destination itself might change along the way.

So, what do you do when your neatly laid plans fray at the edges? You adapt, you improvise, and you keep moving forward. This chapter is dedicated to giving you tips to change your game plan while keeping your eyes on the prize – your ultimate goal.

First, you need to accept that change is part of the process. Even though you need to take a different approach, your goal is still valid and attainable. It's crucial to understand that flexibility is a strength, not a weakness. Being able to adapt to new circumstances means you're resourceful and resilient – two qualities that are invaluable in any endeavor.

Now, let's talk about the practical side of things. How do you go about changing your game plan?

The first step is to reassess your current position. Where are you right now about your goal? Have the circumstances changed? Has new information come to light that affects your journey? Take stock of what's different and why a change might be necessary. This is not an exercise in rationalization for giving up; rather, it is an exercise in facing up to the facts to make good decisions in the future.

Once you've got a clear picture of where you stand, consider your options. There's rarely only one path to success, and flexibility is finding the other routes that can lead you to your destination. This might mean learning new skills, seeking advice from others who've faced similar challenges, or even temporarily setting aside your pride to take a step that seems like it's leading you backward. It's okay—forward progress isn't always a straight line.

Next, you want to adjust your timeline. When the unexpected happens, your original timeline for reaching your goal might no longer be realistic. This isn't a sign of failure; it's an acknowledgment of reality. Permit yourself to set a new timeline, one that's achievable under the new circumstances. This can relieve the pressure and allow you to focus on progress rather than perfection.

Communication is also key. If your plan change affects others – maybe it's a team project, or you have stakeholders in your business – keep them informed. Transparency builds trust, and you'll often find that others are more understanding and supportive than expected. They might even offer help or solutions that you hadn't considered.

Once you've figured out your new approach, commit to it fully. Half-hearted measures are likely to fail to be successful. Dive into the new plan with the same enthusiasm and commitment as you had for the original. This commitment will carry you through the tough moments when doubt and frustration creep in.

Speaking of tough moments, be prepared for them. Changing your game plan takes time and effort. There will be challenges, and there will be moments when you question whether you've made the right choice. When those moments come, remind yourself why you started on this path in the first place. Revisit your original goal and the passion that spurred you to pursue it. That core motivation is your anchor, and it will keep you steady.

And while you're keeping your eyes on your goal, remember to celebrate the small victories along the way. They prove that you're moving in the right direction, no matter how many twists and turns the path might take. These small wins are also incredibly motivating, and they can provide the energy you need to keep going when the going gets tough.

Finally, stay open to continuous learning. The more you learn, the better equipped you are to handle change. Read books, take courses, talk to experts – absorb as much information as possible. Knowledge is power, and the power to adapt is exactly what you need when your plans change.

Remember that being flexible doesn't mean giving up on your dreams. It means being smart enough to navigate the reality of the road to reach those dreams. Changing your game plan isn't a detour; it's part of the journey to success. So, calm yourself, collect your thoughts, and charge headfirst into the new strategy.

By being prepared to change your game plan without losing sight of your goal, you set yourself up not just for success but for a kind of success that is richer and more rewarding because it's been truly earned. The path might be unpredictable, but your determination to reach the end of it will make all the difference. And that, in essence, is the heart of this chapter—understanding that the goal is constant, but the path to it is variable, and that's not just okay; it's expected.

In these pages, we'll walk through this journey together, step by step, with real-life examples, practical advice, and simple yet powerful encouragement to keep you moving towards your dreams, no matter what changes come your way.

Learn how to bounce back and make smart moves when things change

When you start something new or work towards a goal, there's one thing you can count on: things will change. The road from start to finish is never as straight or clear as we hope. But you know what? That's part of the adventure. This chapter is about learning how to handle those changes, not just to survive them but to come out on top, making smart moves that keep you going in the right direction.

Imagine you're on a journey. You have your map, your packed lunch, and your shiny goal in your pocket. You're all set. But then, the weather changes, or the road you walk gets blocked. What do you do? You find another way. That's what life is about—finding another way. This is what this chapter will help you do.

So, let's talk about that – the bouncing back and the making of smart moves. It all starts with how you think about change. See, change is normal. It happens to everyone. It's not a sign that you're doing something wrong or not meant to reach your goal. It's just a sign that you're moving, and movement brings change.

When things change, the first thing you need to do is stop and look around. Take a deep breath. This is where you get to know the new landscape. What's different now? What are the new rules? You've got to understand the game you're playing before you can win it.

Next, it's time to get a little creative. You've got a problem to solve, and solving problems needs creativity. This means thinking about your skills and resources in a new way. There may be a skill you've never thought to use or a friend you've not reached out to. This is your chance to mix things up and try new combinations. It's like cooking – sometimes, the unexpected ingredients make the best dishes.

Now, you've got some ideas about what to do next, but before you jump in, ask yourself: Is this move going to take me closer to my goal? It's easy to make a quick move just because you want to feel like you're doing something, but every move should be a step toward where you want to be. If it's not, it might be time to think again.

Let's say you've got a move in mind that will get you back on track. Great! But before you charge ahead, pause and make a plan. What are the steps? How will you know if it's working?

What will you do if it's not? Making a plan is like drawing a mini-map for your mini-adventure.

With your plan in hand, it's time to take action. This part can be scary because it's real. You're not just thinking or planning; you're doing. Remember to take it one step at a time. You don't have to see the whole road, just the next step. And every step you take is a win, so celebrate it. Pat yourself on the back for having the guts to keep moving.

But what if the step you took didn't work out? That's okay. Failure isn't the opposite of success; it's a part of it. Every time something doesn't work, you learn. And learning is the secret weapon of every successful person. They're not smarter or luckier than anyone else; they learn faster and use what they learn to make better moves next time.

Speaking of next time, always be ready to make your next move. Keep your goal in mind, but keep your eyes on the ground where you're walking. Be ready to zigzag or jump or even turn around if it means getting closer to your goal.

While you're at it, keep talking to people. Share your changes and challenges with friends, family, or mentors. They might see things you don't. They might have ideas you have yet to think of. We're all in this together, and sometimes, the help you need is just a conversation away.

Also, remember to look after yourself. Changing plans and making moves is hard work. Make sure you're eating well, sleeping enough, and taking breaks. A tired you is not the best you, and you need your best you to tackle these challenges.

Finally, keep believing in yourself. You've got this. You've made it this far, and you're still going. That takes real guts. Hold onto the belief that you can do it, even when it's hard, especially when it's hard. That belief is like a light in the dark, showing you the way forward.

Now, that's a lot to take in. But let's boil it down to the essentials: Change happens. Understand it. Get creative. Plan smart. Take action. Celebrate every step. Learn from failure. Make your next move. Talk about it. Look after yourself. Believe in yourself.

Remember, every change is a chance to show how flexible, creative, and resilient you can be. It's a chance to learn something new and get closer to your goal. So embrace it, tackle it, and let it take you somewhere even better than you planned.

In the pages to follow, we'll break down these steps with stories of people just like you who faced change head-on and came out winners. We'll give you the nitty-gritty on how to turn setbacks into comebacks. By the end of this chapter, you'll not just be ready for change; you'll be looking forward to it. Because you'll know that change is not the end of your journey—it's just a twist in the story. And who doesn't love a good twist? It's what makes the story worth reading.

CHAPTER 10

TOUGHING IT OUT

In this Chapter Toughing It out This is where we get to the real talk about resilience and grit. Life is like a marathon, not a sprint. It's long, it's hard, and there are times when you want to stop and sit down. But here's the thing: it's also incredibly rewarding, especially when you push through the hard bits and keep going.

In this chapter, we will look at what it means to tough it out. This is about more than sticking with something when it gets a little tricky. It's about what you do when facing obstacles that feel like mountains when you're so tired you can hardly think, or when everything seems to be telling you to give up.

You might wonder, "How do I keep going when I feel like I can't?" Well, that's exactly what we'll explore. You'll find out that you're stronger than you think and have more in your tank than you realize. Toughness isn't just about physical strength. It's about the strength inside your head and your heart.

We'll share stories of people who have been right where you are and pushed through. They're not superheroes; they're regular folks like you and me, but they've found ways to keep their feet moving, one step at a time, even when those steps felt impossible.

And we'll give you some practical advice, too. How do you make a tough decision? What do you tell yourself when you feel like quitting? How do you find the energy to start each day positively, even when yesterday knocked you down? We'll cover all that and more.

Most importantly, this chapter is about hope. It's about the light at the end of the tunnel and that you're closer to it than you think. It's about learning that toughness is not about never falling; it's about how you get up after you fall.

So, take a deep breath. We're about to dive in. Remember, this chapter is a tool for you—a companion for those tough times. Use it whenever you need it because no matter what, you need to know that you can tough it out. You've got this.

How to keep your cool when things get tricky

In life, there are times when things get so tricky and complicated that we feel like we're trying to walk through a brick wall. It's like you're trying to keep your cool, but inside, you're just a pot ready to boil over. We all know that feeling. First up, it's important to realize that everyone has these moments. It's not just you. And the folks who seem to glide through trouble? They've just gotten good at dealing with problems, that's all. They're not different or special; they've just had a lot of practice. And good news — you can get good at it, too.

When something hard smacks you in the face, your first reaction might be to smack right back. But hold on a second. Take a deep breath. Count to ten. Do whatever you need to do to stop for a moment. This tiny pause can give you just enough time to stop a bad situation from getting worse.

Now, look at what's in front of you. What's the problem here? Break it down. When you look at it closely, it might be smaller than you first thought. And even if it is big, once you've broken it down into smaller pieces, you can tackle it bit by bit instead of all at once.

Next, remember you don't have to do it alone. It's okay to ask for help. There are people out there who've been through what you're going through, and most of them are happy to give you a hand or some advice. You have to reach out. It could be a friend, a family member, someone at work, or even an online forum.

Another thing — keep your eyes on the prize. Why are you doing this? What's the goal? Sometimes, remembering why you started can give you the strength to keep going. Write it down if that helps. Stick it on your wall. Make it your phone's wallpaper.

Keep it close to remind yourself that there's a reason for all this effort.

Let's remember to celebrate the little wins, too. Did you get through a tough conversation without losing your cool? That's a win. Did you figure out even one small part of the problem? Another win Celebrate that. It's proof you're moving forward, even if it's just a little bit.

And here's something super important: know when to take a break. When you're stressed, everything feels impossible. Sometimes, the best thing you can do is step away for a bit. Go for a walk. Listen to some music. It's not quitting — it's recharging.

Also, be kind to yourself. You wouldn't yell at a friend having a tough time, right? So, could you not do it to yourself? Talk to yourself like you would to a buddy, Encouraging words can make a huge difference.

But what about those times when things don't work out, no matter how hard you try? It happens. And it's rough. But it's not the end of the world. When something doesn't go your way, it's a chance to learn. It might not feel like it right then, but every mistake, every setback, has something to teach you. And that's valuable.

Now, let's be clear: keeping your cool isn't about never getting mad or upset. It's about managing those feelings so they don't run the show. It's okay to be frustrated. It's okay to be disappointed. It's what you do next that counts.

Let's say you're working on something, and it's just not happening. You've tried everything, and it's just not working. You're at boiling point. Instead of giving up or blowing up, take that break we discussed. Then come back and try something different. There may be another way to solve the problem, a way you haven't thought of yet.

And remember, the tricky times are when you grow the most. It's like working out. The first time you lift weights, it's tough, and you're sore the next day. But if you keep at it, you get stronger. It's the same with problems. The more you face them, the better you get at it, and the less they scare you.

So, when things get tricky, take that breath. Break down the problem. Ask for help. Focus on why you're doing it. Celebrate the little wins. Take a break if you need it. Be kind to yourself. Learn from the setbacks. Try new solutions. And through it all, keep believing in yourself.

That's how you keep your cool when the heat is on. It's not about never feeling the heat; it's about learning to dance in the flames. And you can. You've got everything you need right inside you. Just take it one step at a time.

We'll talk about ways to stay pumped and focused on your goal

Staying pumped and focused on your goal is like trying to keep a fire burning on a windy day. You've got to protect it, feed it, and sometimes you've got to rekindle it. In this piece, we'll talk about how to keep that fire – your drive and focus – alive, even when life throws a bucket of water over it.

Imagine you've got this big, bright goal in front of you. It gets you out of bed in the morning and keeps you up late at night. But let's be real: keeping your eye on the prize is sometimes a walk in the park. There will be days when the couch calls your name, and your goal seems a million miles away. What do you do then?

Well, first off, you have to remember why you started. This isn't just any goal; it's *your* goal. It means something to you, right? Keep that 'why' at the forefront of your mind. You could write it down, put it on your fridge, or set it as a reminder on your phone. When you remember why you're chasing this dream, it becomes a lot harder to ignore.

Now, let's talk about routine. Routine is like the unsung hero of focus. You do the same things at the same times, and soon, they become a part of who you are. It's not about being rigid but about creating a rhythm for your life that keeps you moving toward what you want, even on autopilot.

But you're not a robot. And that's where the human part comes in - you have to spice it up sometimes. Change your surroundings, tweak your schedule, or throw a new challenge. This keeps your brain on its toes and can reenergize your commitment to your goal.

Talking about energy, who are you hanging out with? Are they the wind in your sails or the anchor dragging you down? Surround yourself with cheerleaders, with people who get it, who cheer on your every step, and who pick you up when you stumble. Their energy can fuel your own, and suddenly, that goal doesn't seem so far away.

But even the best of us get sidetracked. You could start a side project, or life throws a curveball that demands your attention. It happens. Instead of beating yourself up about it, look at the big picture. Is this new thing in line with your ultimate goal? Can it enrich your journey instead of distracting from it? Sometimes, these 'distractions' can be blessings in disguise, offering new ways to approach our goals.

However, let's not kid ourselves; there will be days when you can't even. You're tired, you're fed up, and the sofa is whispering sweet nothings in your ear. What then? Give yourself a break. A real one. It's not a 'scroll through social media' break, but something that truly rejuvenates you. Read a book, go for a run, play with your dog, or just nap. Rest is not the enemy of progress; it's a part of it.

Let's also remember the power of celebrating the small stuff. Every little step towards your goal is worth a happy dance. Have you finished a task Great, Overcame a hurdle? Fantastic. Each of these victories is like a log on your fire, burning your motivation brightly.

And what about when you miss the mark? When you fall flat on your face? That's not the time to throw in the towel. It's the time to look for the lesson. What went wrong? How can you do it differently next time? This isn't failure; it's school, and every lesson makes you smarter and stronger.

One thing we still need to talk about is the naysayers. You know, the ones – who doubt, criticize, and roll their eyes. Listen, the only reason to pay them any mind is to use their doubt as fuel. Prove them wrong. Let their disbelief be the thing that makes you push even harder.

But while you're pushing, remember to keep things fun. Yes, goals are serious business, but they don't have to be joyless. Inject fun into the process. Make a game out of your tasks, celebrate in silly ways, and laugh at the absurdity when things go sideways. Fun isn't just for kids – it's a fantastic way to stay engaged in what you're doing.

Persistence doesn't mean you never stop; it means you always start again. That goal is still there, waiting for you. And every day you chip away at it, you get closer.

Remember, staying pumped and focused isn't a one-time deal. It's a series of choices you make every day. It's about the little things as much as the big things. It's about knowing that the fire – your drive – is inside you, and only you can decide whether to let it burn out or blaze a trail toward your dreams. So, feed it, protect it, rekindle it when necessary, and watch as you turn your goals into reality.

CHAPTER 11

THINK DIFFERENT, THINK BIG

Sometimes, the usual way of thinking just doesn't cut it. If you're going to reach for the stars, you've got to stand on your toes, stretch your arms, and jump a little. That's what thinking big is all about.

In this chapter, we're not just going to chat about thinking outside the box; we're going to throw the box away. It's about shaking how you see things, turning them on your head, and asking, 'What if?' The same old thinking gets you the same old results, and we're after something new, something bigger.

We'll explore how different kinds of thinking can lead to big ideas. How asking simple questions can unlock creativity, and how looking at things from another person's shoes can give you a whole new perspective. You'll learn how some folks, maybe just like you, started with a small thought and grew it into something huge.

But don't worry, thinking big doesn't mean thinking complicated. We'll keep it simple because sometimes the biggest ideas are the easiest to understand. They need someone to believe in them enough to see them grow.

So, buckle up. It's time to broaden our horizons and let our minds explore the possibilities Who knows what we'll come up with when we give ourselves the chance to think differently and think big?

Learn to use your skill in ways no one else has thought of

At the point when you take a gander at experts, regardless of the field they're in, there is by all accounts a consistent idea that integrates their encounters: they continue onward, particularly when things get complicated. The unavoidable issue is: how would they make it happen? How would they push past the problematic stretches to make progress?

We should investigate how these geniuses can continue to the end whenever hard times arise.

Most importantly, experts comprehend that difficulties are essential for the excursion. They realize that each impediment isn't a barrier but a venting stone. They utilize these difficulties as learning to open doors, developing from everyone. When confronted with trouble, rather than surrendering, they ask themselves what they can gain from the circumstance and how it can improve them at what they do.

How precisely do they handle these issues? First off, they keep their eyes on the objective. This implies they have a reasonable comprehension of what they need to accomplish. It's not just about having a fantasy or a wish. It's tied in with having a dream so distinctive and clear that it feels genuine to them, even before they've accomplished it. This clarity assists them with staying on track and not getting diverted by brief difficulties.

Experts likewise know the worth of a solid, emotionally supportive network. They have areas of strength for a framework comprised of family, companions, guides, and friends who are consistently there to support them, offer sound exhortation, and listen closely when needed. In some cases, individuals need the help of those near them to continue to go when times are harsh.

Presently, how would they manage disappointment? Indeed, stars don't see disappointment in the manner in which the vast majority do. For their purposes, disappointment isn't something contrary to progress; it's essential for progress. That's what they grasp if they're not flopping sporadically; they likely need to propel themselves harder. Along these lines, they accept every disappointment, gain from it, and use it to illuminate their following stages.

One more critical component is their capacity to remain trained and constant. Experts set up schedules and stick to them in any event when not in that frame of mind. They appear daily, accomplish the work, and focus on their art. This discipline gathers speed after some time and prompts forward leaps.

With regards to critical thinking, masters have an exciting methodology. They divide the problem into more modest, reasonable parts to stay calm. Along these lines, they can handle each section in turn, which makes the case manageable but rather more resolvable.

Flexibility is another attribute that makes all the difference for experts. They're available to change and able to turn when essential. If one methodology isn't working, they're sufficiently adaptable to start something new. This deftness permits them to explore through questionable times without becoming lost.

Geniuses likewise put resources into their abilities and information ceaselessly. They're long-lasting students, continuously hoping to improve and remain refreshed in their field. This obligation to learn guarantees they have the devices and understanding to overcome obstructions.

As far as mentality, experts keep an uplifting perspective. They're positive thinkers who trust that what is going on can be convoluted, regardless of how intense. This doesn't mean they're guileless or disregard reality. It implies they center around what they have some control over and stay confident about the result.

Besides, they deal with their energy carefully. Stars realize that they can't go at maximum speed constantly. They perceive the significance of rest and recovery and incorporate time into their timetables to re-energize. This assists them with keeping up with their endurance over an extended period.

Quite possibly, the main thing that stars do is commend the little wins en route. Their confidence and drive are helped by their acknowledgment and festivity of their accomplishments. Perceiving these little triumphs advises them that they are pushing ahead, in any event, when progress feels slow.

Finally, experts are energetic about what they do. This energy powers their drive and responsibility. It gets them up in the first part of the day and keeps them burning the midnight oil. At the point when you love what you do, enduring through difficult stretches becomes more straightforward.

What pushes the experts along is a blend of clarity, support, gaining from disappointment, discipline, critical thinking, versatility, ceaseless learning, inspiration, energy for the board, commending progress, and enthusiasm. They don't have a mysterious equation or an enchanted wand that makes difficulties vanish. They have a bunch of perspectives and ways of behaving that they practice reliably.

Understanding these procedures and attitudes is only the initial step. When you begin utilizing them, that is the point at which the magic occurs. Thus, contemplate your objectives and the difficulties you're confronting. Consider combining these expert approaches to dealing with challenges and keeping going when things get crazy. Remember, it's not necessary to focus on being great or never confronting troubles; it's about how you answer those hardships and advance toward your desires.

We'll check out how some people used their skills to do cool new things

At the point when you ponder abilities and how individuals use them, similar to a money box, a great many people possibly take two or three coins from when there's sufficient to make them rich. You have an expertise, perhaps more than one—yet would you say you are utilizing it to its maximum capacity?

There are endless accounts of people who took straightforward expertise and bent it into something astonishing, something that made them stick out. These aren't only stories to tell around a pit fire; they're genuine motivations that show us what's conceivable when we inspire us to think bigger a bit.

Take the narrative of Sarah, for instance. She cherished baking. It was an expertise she had sharpened since she was a young lady helping her grandmother in the kitchen. For a long time, Sarah heated for her family companions, even at nearby local area occasions. Yet, that was all there was to it. It was only a side interest; she got along admirably, yet she hadn't pondered taking it further.

Then, at some point, her companion, adversely affected by nuts, was annoyed about not finding delectable sans nut-heated merchandise. It struck Sarah that there should be such countless individuals like her companion. Along these lines, she began testing. She utilized her baking abilities to make recipes that were sans nut yet tasty. She started a blog, shared her recipes, and in what would seem like no time, she had a following. Individuals from everywhere were requesting her heated products. Sarah took her essential expertise and filled a hole on the lookout. She's running a fruitful bread shop caring for individuals with food sensitivities.

Or on the other hand, think about Mike, a visual planner with a sharp eye for detail. He worked for a little organization, making promotions and handouts. Yet, beyond work, he cherished playing with his kids and making elaborate coloring books for them. He began sharing his plans via virtual entertainment, and they grabbed the attention of a distributor. They were unique—mind-boggling and unpredictable, not your standard youngsters' toll. They were shading books that grown-ups cherished since they were testing and unwinding simultaneously. Mike's side venture transformed into a subsequent work. He used his expertise in visual depiction to make something for something else altogether.

Then there's Priya, who had a skill for dialects. She could get a language's nuts and bolts by paying attention to it for a couple of days. Priya worked in travel service, yet she utilized her language abilities to begin a YouTube channel to share speedy and simple language-learning tips for explorers, which started as a little undertaking turned into her full-time gig. She presently works with the travel industry sheets and language learning applications, and she's transformed her ability into a thrilling profession that fills her energy for movement.

At the point when we discuss abilities, it's about more than whatever you're great at. It's about how you use what you're great at. It resembles having a kitchen loaded with fixings; sure, you could make the typical, worn-out dishes consistently or investigate concocting something previously unheard of.

Take James, for example. He was a standard person who knew everything there was to know about PCs. He wasn't a programmer or anything. However, he could deal with the common IT issues. He understood that numerous more established people in his area were continuously worrying over PC issues. They didn't grow up with innovation as he did, so he saw an opportunity to help. James began free end-of-the-week classes at the nearby public venue, teaching seniors how to utilize PCs, the web, and online entertainment. In addition to the fact that he helped his neighbors, however, he likewise began a not-for-profit that extended to a few urban communities.

Says like these show us that our abilities can have a lot greater effect than we naturally suspect. It's tied in with taking a gander at what we know how to do and afterward driving it further, asking, 'How else could I at any point manage this?'

Anyway, shouldn't something be said about you? What expertise do you have that could be transformed into something exceptional? You might be great at drawing, and you could begin making custom works of art for individuals' pets. Or, on the other hand, you're a pro at fixing bicycles, and you could start a portable fix administration.

Also, don't think you want to stop your average employment to make something else of your abilities. Begin little, and see where it goes. Many fruitful organizations and tasks began as part-time jobs or side interests. You may be perched on a mother lode and not even know it.

The key is to check your abilities out diversely. Try not to agree with how you've generally managed them. Push the limits. Ponder what individuals need or what might make their lives more straightforward or joyful. Your abilities can overcome that issue.

Remember that each individual who utilized their expertise to accomplish something cool and new needed to begin someplace. They made that first dubious stride; they put themselves out there and attempted. Only one out of every odd endeavor transformed into an example of overcoming adversity; however, they gained from each insight and continued onward.

Thus, pause for a minute to contemplate your range of abilities. What are you great at? What do you adore doing? Presently, blend that in with a bit of boldness to have a go at a new thing, add a sprinkle of creative mind, and see what you can concoct. The most terrible that can happen is you'll have a decent story to tell. You could wind up like Sarah, Mike, Priya, or James, utilizing your abilities to cool new things inside the world, perhaps the past.

There's an entire scene of chance so those willing can unexpectedly see their abilities. It's about being willing to try, to blend and match, to change and contort. What's more, all the while, you'll advance your own life, yet you could likewise bring something new and brilliant into the existences of others.

Eventually, that is what's going on with it. Utilizing what we have, know, and are enthusiastic about will have an effect. So go on, take your ability, and stir it up. Use it to open entryways you didn't know were there. And afterward, step through and perceive how the world opens up accordingly. That is where the genuine experience starts.

CHAPTER 12

SHARE THE MAGIC TEACHING YOUR SKILL

While you've worked hard to analyze something and are appropriate at it, it's like having a superpower. Consider you double that superpower's strength by sharing it with someone else. That is what this chapter is all about: the multiplying impact of coaching your talent.

You have spent hours together with your nostrils in textbooks, solving problem after trouble until the numbers dance to your desires. You have to take care of it, and now you're the go-to individual while friends need assistance with their math homework. Have you considered taking a step similarly and coaching a math magnificence as a volunteer or a coach? Here's why that might be a high-quality concept.

Firstly, teaching places you instantly. You have to be clear in your mind to make it clear to someone else. It would help if you got your mind to simplify demanding standards into workable chunks. This, in turn, deepens your knowledge and, once in a while, even well-known information shows gaps in your understanding that you could then fill.

Secondly, students often ask questions you need to learn about yourself. This may lead you to consider your talents from specific angles. It challenges you to examine what you realize in a new light to discover areas you might have omitted.

Thirdly, there is something about seeing someone else get it for the first time—that 'aha!' moment while their face lights up because they have grasped an idea. It is profitable. It could reignite your ardor for your skill, especially if you've hit a plateau or feel a bit burned out.

However, it's not just about the coaching itself. It's approximately the coaching, too. To teach, you need to prepare, and education means reading. It approaches becoming even more acquainted with your ability, gaining knowledge of new strategies, or discovering more modern, less complicated ways to explain it. You'll recognize the problem better than you ever did before.

Reflect on consideration of the people you'll meet adequately. Coaching is always a -way road. Your students will come from different backgrounds with distinct perspectives. They may share their experiences and expertise simply as you share your abilities. It's an exchange, and in that exchange, you may grow.

You may be exposed to new facts which could enhance your information and outlook on lifestyles.

Moreover, teaching is ability in itself. It's about communication, patience, empathy, and management. Growing these gentle skills can help you in all areas of life, from your professional profession to your relationships. By teaching, you are now not only a master of your craft but also a master of interacting with others.

Now, you are probably questioning, "What if I am no longer a professional? What if I don't know sufficient?" That's the splendor of it. You won't be a person apart from the world's leading authority on a subject to teach it. You want to recognize enough to help someone else take their first steps. Remember, to a fourth-grader, a fifth-grader is a professional in '5th-grade stuff.' it's all approximately context.

There are infinite stories of those who began teaching something as a way to offer it again or just as a side gig and it changed their lives. The music instructor started by giving classes in her residing room and motivated an era of musicians in her town. The retired engineer volunteered at a nearby faculty and determined a renewed sense of motive. Their memories aren't just about the teaching but also about the network they constructed the lives they touched, and the pride they observed.

So, where do you begin? Look around your community for opportunities. Is there a community center that might use a volunteer to lead a workshop? A local library wherein you can host a talk or a class? How about online platforms where humans continually try to analyze new things? The possibilities are there, waiting for you to grab them.

In this chapter, you'll learn the steps to begin coaching your ability, from the logistics of finding a platform to the finer points of crafting your first lesson plan. We will talk about how to engage with students, handle the challenges that include teaching, and hold matters amusing and exciting for each of you and your students.

Via the give-up of this chapter, teaching isn't always giving; it is approximately exchanging. It's an adventure that could take your skill—and you—to places you by no means anticipated. It is a pathway to not simply becoming higher at what you do but turning into a better you. So, let's dive in and explore how you can begin sharing your magic with the sector, one lesson at a time.

Get tips on sharing your skill without a sweat

When you've got something cool that you can do, like cook mean lasagna, draw a portrait that could almost wink at you, or solve math problems like they're riddles, there's a pretty neat thing you can do with it – teach it to someone else. Now, sharing what you know can seem a bit daunting at first. But it's like riding a bike – shaky at the start, but before you know it, you're cruising. So, let's get into how you can pass on your skills without breaking a sweat.

First things first, don't make it a big deal. You don't need to stand in front of a crowd with a microphone or anything. Start small. You could be showing a friend how to whip up your signature dish while they're over at your place. The trick is to keep it casual. Chat about what you're doing, like telling them about a good movie you saw. Keep it friendly and simple.

Now, when you decide to take someone under your wing, remember you're not trying to turn them into a mini-you. You're just giving them the tools to start their journey. So when you teach, teach them the basics – those first little steps that got you hooked. Like if you're teaching guitar, show them how to hold the thing without getting a cramp. Don't jump straight into the fancy finger-work. Walk before you run, right?

Here's something many folks don't tell you – it's okay to mess up. If you're showing someone how to fix a bike and you drop a screw, laugh it off. It shows them that everyone – even the person teaching them – can make mistakes. It makes the whole thing a lot less serious and fun.

Let's talk about the tools of the trade. You don't need the top-of-the-line gear to teach someone. If you're into photography, you don't need the newest camera to show someone the ropes. Use what you have, and show them that they can start with whatever they've got. It's the skill that counts, not the equipment.

You've got your own story about getting into this thing you're good at. Share that. Maybe you started baking because your grandma's cookies were the bomb, or you used a camera to capture moments like no other. When you weave in your tale, it's not just a lesson – it's a conversation. And that's when the person learning from you gets invested.

Listening is just as important as talking when you're teaching. Watch the person learning. Do they look confused? Are they getting it? If they're lost, find a new way to explain. Use different words or show them again. And if they nail it, that's your cue to give them a high-five.

Patience is your best friend here. If they don't get it the first time, or the second, or even the third, it's cool. Think about how long it took you to get good. They'll get there; they need time. Be the person who gives them that time.

Encouragement is like sunshine for people learning something new. It makes them grow. So, be generous with your "hey, that's looking great!" comments. It builds their confidence, and that's half the battle won.

Remember that the moment you start teaching, you're signing up for a refresher course yourself. There's always something new to discover about your skill, and often, it's while you're teaching it. Embrace that. It keeps your passion fresh.

Teaching isn't just about passing on your skills. It's about people. You are connecting with them, understanding them, and having a blast with them. Those moments when things go a little sideways, and you both laugh. That's the good stuff.

Feedback isn't just for the learner; it's for you, too. Ask them how you're doing. It'll help you get better at explaining things, and it'll make your lessons even cooler.

Be sure to complete the hard parts. Sharing the struggle is important. It shows that the road isn't always smooth, but that's alright. The bumps are where you learn the most, after all.

When you get your learner involved, that's when the magic happens. If you're teaching coding, doesn't just code in front of them; get them to type out the lines, too. They'll remember it better if they do it themselves.

Remember, teaching isn't a sprint; it's more of a scenic road trip. There's no finish line, so you can keep going, teaching, and making those connections.

Finally, give it your spin. Share why this skill lights you up. Is it the way flour, eggs, and sugar turn into a cake? Or how a few lines on paper turn into a face? Whatever your reason, let it shine through. That passion is contagious, and it's what will inspire someone else to love what they do just as much as you do.

So there you go. Sharing your skill isn't about being perfect or having all the answers. It's about being real, being patient, and being willing to jump in and have some fun. When you do that, you're not just teaching someone how to do something – you're giving them a little piece of the thing that makes you, well, you.

CHAPTER 13

SHOW ME THE MONEY MAKING YOUR SKILL PAY

Imagine being good at something, like baking cakes that make people's taste buds sing or being able to program like a wizard. They did it for fun, for their friends, or just for themselves. But then I realized I could make money with this.

This chapter is like the day I set up my first lemonade stand as a kid. It's not just lemon and sugar. You have skills that will be rewarded. Let's look at how you can turn your favorite activity into more than just a hobby. We explore how to get started, find people to pay for your offer, and keep the money flowing.

But this isn't just about making money. It's the smart thing to do. We're not talking about get-rich-quick schemes here. We're talking about the real thing: doing quality work with your hands (or brains!) and making honest money.

Whether you're thinking of selling your craft, offering your services as a freelancer, or even teaching your skills to others for a fee, this chapter has you covered.

Turn your skill into cash with these smart moves

Do you realize that thing you do nearly automatically? It may be doodling characters that could have a place in a comic book, repairing old bicycles until they're all around great, or preparing dinner with your companions and asking for the recipe. Consider the possibility that I let you know that you could transform that skill into some genuine cash. Let's discuss how that is conceivable.

Priorities aside, we should become genuinely concerned about what this implies. We're not looking at getting up tomorrow swimming in a heap of cash like you've scored in that sweepstakes. No, this is tied in with seeing what you're great at and tracking down savvy ways of procuring it. Prettyany expertise can be adapted on the off chance that you approach it accurately. Moreover, that begins with seeing your expertise through a business focal point.

Take Sarah, for example. She adores making beaded adornments. It began as a side interest to loosen up after her average everyday employment. However, at that point, her companions began asking where they could get her manifestations. That is the point at which the light went off. Sarah acknowledged she could sell her adornments. She began little, setting up an internet-based shop and sharing her pieces via web-based entertainment. Individuals cherished her work, and in a flash, orders were coming in quicker than she could string globules.

Yet, perhaps you're thinking, "That is perfect for Sarah, yet what might be said about me?" The key is to begin seeing your expertise as a help or item that takes care of an issue for individuals. Perhaps you're perfect with numbers and can assist private ventures with their records, or maybe you're a wiz with tech issues and could offer IT support.

It would help to spread the news whenever you've sorted out how your expertise can help others. Nowadays, that involves typically signing onto the web. There are a few spots online where individuals who could profit from your administrations could track down you, including virtual entertainment, fundamental sites, and commercial centers. It resembles setting up a virtual lemonade stand where the world strolls by.

Then, at that point, there's value. This can be a tightrope walk since you must figure out that perfect balance where individuals will pay for your expertise without feeling cheated. A decent starting spot is looking at what others charge for comparable administrations or items. It's OK to begin at a lower cost and raise your rates as you get more insight and interest in your work.

We should discuss developing what you've begun. The informal exchange can be your dearest companion whenever you have a couple of blissful clients. Urge people to get the message out. Offer a markdown on their next buy if they get new clients. Also, watch out for what they say regarding your work - input resembles gold residue, making what you offer far superior.

Yet, what might be said about when things get a piece rough? Arrange delayed down or a recent fad implies you must adjust what you offer. This is the point at which it's significant to be adaptable and imaginative. For instance, if you're a fitness coach and individuals are unexpectedly about yoga, why not get confirmed and add yoga classes to your collection?

Another savvy move is to continue to learn. Regardless of how great you are, there's continuously a genuinely new thing to get that can make your business more grounded. It may be a course in web-based showcasing, or it's simply keeping steady over recent fads in your field.

Every one of these requires some investment and exertion. You will just now and again need to go through your nights or ends of the week dealing with your second job. Yet, the magnificence of transforming your ability into cash is that it's not just about the money. It's tied in with accomplishing and getting compensated for something you love. There's something unbelievably fulfilling about that.

However, how about we recall the legitimate side of things? As things get, you'll need to guarantee you're getting everything done right - covering charges, obtaining any essential licenses or allows, and setting up as an authority business. It sounds overwhelming, yet there are numerous assets to assist you with getting everything arranged.

At long last, make sure to take in the scenery. Of course, the additional money is perfect, yet this is likewise about the excitement of creating something from nothing, being your chief, and getting better at what you do daily.

Transforming your ability into cash involves mixing energy with common sense. It's an excursion with promising and less promising times; however, for those ready to invest the effort, it can be taken care of in additional ways than one. Whether it's adornments, assessment forms, or yoga, the world is hanging tight for that extraordinary thing you can offer. So go on, take those savvy actions, and watch as your ability becomes something that can cover the bills.

Learn to make the most of your skill in the big wide world

Imagine you have this one thing you're great at. Perhaps you're the individual who can recount stories that stick everybody to their seats, or you have a talent for making contraptions work when every other person will surrender and toss them through the window. You have expertise, old buddy, and I'm here to let you know that there's a significant world out there only hanging tight for somebody like you to move forward and sparkle.

You're presumably thinking, "Sure, I'm great at this, yet how would I get from being great in my own little corner to taking advantage of it out there?" That is where the excursion gets fascinating.

Most importantly, have confidence in your ability. This isn't tied in with puffing your chest out and gloating. About realizing where it counts, you have something that would merit offering. It resembles when you recognize a mystery that will better fill everybody's heart with joy — you're anxious to share it. That is how you ought to feel about your abilities.

Then, significantly improve at it. All in all, hurl yourself entirely into it. Practice it, refine it, and learn about it until it's relaxing. Why? The world is brimming with individuals who are very significant at bunches of things, yet the ones who stand out are the ones who are perfect at a specific something. They're the ones we recall, the ones we return to, and the ones we discuss.

Presently, here's where it gets enjoyable. It would help if you put yourself out there. Suppose you're a virtuoso at visual depiction. Begin sharing your work. Could you put it on the web? Show it to companions—volunteer for projects. Every little step puts your expertise out there more, and each time somebody sees what you can do, that is a seed planted.

Furthermore, don't simply adhere to what you know. Search for better approaches to push your abilities out into the world. That could mean showing others or involving your expertise in a manner no other person has considered at this point. If you're a fantastic pie producer around, have a go at showing a class or selling your pies at a neighborhood market. At the point when you stretch yourself, you don't simply develop your ability — you build your chances.

Putting yourself out there comes the unnerving part: analysis. Only some people will cherish what you do, which is not a problem. It's more than alright — it's perfect. Why? Since input is how you improve. Stand by listening to what individuals express, filter through it for the valuable pieces, and use it to clean your ability until it sparkles.

Then, at that point, you must begin pondering the quick and dirty. That implies sorting out whether or not there's a method for making some money from your expertise. It's excellent overall to be perfect at something; however, if you can transform that into a check, why couldn't you? It very well may be selling your specialty, it very well may be outsourcing as an afterthought, or it very well may be finding some work that needs precisely the exact thing you're best at.

However, remember that there are better ways to gauge how you're taking advantage of your expertise in the enormous wide world than cash. Each time somebody benefits from what you do that is esteem. That is influence. You could be filling somebody's heart with joy, making some work more straightforward, making a second paramount — that is all essential for it.

Here is a major one: associations. Capitalizing on your expertise is not an independent mission. It would help if you formed an organization of individuals who know your work and value. These are individuals who'll suggest you, hit you up whenever there's an open door, and uphold you when you have a go at a new thing. It resembles being essential for a group where everybody needs another person to win.

Furthermore, it would help if you were steady. The world's noisy, and everybody's attempting to be heard. So you must keep at it, continue appearing, and continue to put your ability out there. Now and again, it'll feel like no one's focusing. That is the point at which you must dig profoundly and continue to go because that isolates the people who make it from those who don't.

Yet, while you're out there taking full advantage of your expertise, don't remember to appreciate it. This isn't just about progress or acknowledgment or cash. It's tied in with making every moment count. At the point when you find euphoria in your work, it follows through in your career, which the world can't resist the urge to answer.

To wrap this up, taking full advantage of your expertise in the large wide world is about something other than something specific. It's tied in with trusting in what you do, getting so great they can't disregard you, putting yourself out there, gaining from the great and the terrible, making associations, persevering, and — in particular — adoring consistently. Your expertise is a gift to you and to every individual who will encounter it.

CHAPTER 14

BE KNOWN FOR WHAT YOU DO BEST

Creating a name for yourself isn't just about getting people to remember who you are; it's about leaving a mark, an imprint that stands for something more. It's about becoming a symbol of excellence in your chosen field, a beacon for others who aspire to reach the heights you've climbed. But this journey isn't for the faint-hearted. It requires more than just being good at what you do—it demands that you embody the skill or trait you wish to be known for.

Let's get down to brass tacks. When you think about creating a name for yourself, what's the first thing that comes to mind? Is it fame? Is it respect? Or it's the satisfaction of knowing you're at the top of your game. Whatever your goal is, the path to creating that name begins with self-awareness. You've got to know yourself inside out—what you're good at, what you love doing, and how you do it differently.

Once you have that self-awareness, the next step is to get to work. And I'm not talking about just any kind of work. I'm talking about the kind that makes you forget time, the kind that challenges you, stretches you, and, ultimately, the kind that fulfills you. This work will define you, but it won't define itself. You've got to put in the time, the effort, and the heart. Because when you pour your whole self into your work, it starts to reflect who you are. It starts to have your name written all over it in invisible ink that only becomes visible through dedication.

Now, you're not just working in silence. You're sharing your progress, your breakthroughs, and even your setbacks. Sharing is powerful—it's how you connect with others, how you get feedback, and how you keep growing. Use the tools at your disposal. Maybe it's social media, maybe it's community events, or maybe it's good old word of mouth. The point is to get your name out there, tied tightly to the quality of work you do. You want people to hear your name and think, "Ah yes, that's the person who knows their stuff."

But here's a key point—consistency. You can't be a one-hit wonder and expect to create a lasting name. You've got to keep delivering, shining, and being the person others can rely on to bring their A-game every single time. Consistency is what builds trust, and trust is what builds a name that sticks.

Now, let's talk about the people you surround yourself with. They say you're the average of the five people you spend the most time with, and there's truth to that. You want to be around people who push you, who believe in your vision, and who are just as committed to excellence as you are. These people will champion your name when you're not in the room. And those conversations—they matter. They're the undercurrents that can lift your name to places you can't reach alone.

As your name grows, so will opportunities. And with opportunities come decisions. What will you say yes to? What will you turn down? These choices will steer the course of your name's voyage. Say yes to things that align with your vision, that challenge you in new ways, and that offer platforms for your name to echo further. Turn down the things that don't serve that vision, that dilute your brand, or that distract you from your path. It's not about being everywhere; it's about being where it counts.

In this game of names, remember to give back. Teaching, mentoring, and sharing your journey not only reinforces your standing but also deepens your understanding of your craft. When you help others, you solidify your status as an expert, as someone worth knowing and remembering. It's a cycle of giving and receiving that feeds the growth of your name.

And finally, be prepared for the long haul. Names aren't made overnight. They're crafted through days, months, and years of consistent, passionate, focused work. They're shaped by the feedback you listen to, the critics you prove wrong, and the fans you delight. It's a marathon, not a sprint, and every step you take builds a legacy.

Creating a name for yourself is crafting a story that others will tell long after you've left the room. It's about being synonymous with something bigger than yourself, about becoming a lighthouse that guides others in the rough seas of your field. Be bold, be patient, be persistent, and watch as your name grows from a whisper to a shout in the halls of your chosen domain.

Use the internet to tell the world about your awesome skill

The internet is like this massive megaphone waiting for you to pick it up and start shouting out about what you're good at. But you can't just start yelling into the void and expect folks to pay attention. You've got to be more clever about it.

First things first, think about where people hang out online. You've got social media sites, blogs, forums, and video platforms. Each one of these is like a different stage in a giant talent show where you get to perform. But every stage has its own rules. You wouldn't attend a poetry slam and start breaking out dance moves. So, you've got to tailor your act—your skill—to fit the stage.

Take social media, for instance. This is where you can get super creative. It's like hosting a mini-exhibition of your skill every single day. Snap a photo, shoot a video, write a post—whatever works for your talent. And make it snappy. People scroll through feeds faster than a kid late for school, so you must make your content pop. Make it so eye-catching that they must stop and see what you're all about.

Now, what if writing's your thing? Blogs are your best friend. With a blog, you get more space to spread out and show off your skills with words. It's like inviting people over to your place for a chat. You can tell stories, share experiences, and dish out advice. The key is to keep it regular. You want folks to keep coming back, like a TV show they can't stop watching.

And let's remember video platforms. If your skill is something people need to see to believe, then videos are the way to go. You may be a whiz at fixing cars, a makeup genius, or you can play guitar like nobody's business. Shoot a video that shows off that talent, and make it fun. Teach something, share tips, or show off what you can do. People love to watch others who are great at what they do—it's inspiring.

Now, maybe you're thinking, "But what if I'm not a social butterfly or a wordsmith?" That's where forums and online communities come in. Find a group that's all about what you love to do. It could be anything from cooking to coding to crafting. In these groups, just be yourself. Ask questions, answer others, and share your work. It's like joining a club where everyone's into the same stuff you are. It feels good, and it gets your name out there.

No matter what platforms you choose, the golden rule is to be genuine. Don't try to be someone you're not just to get likes or follows. It's exhausting, and people can smell fakeness a mile away. Be real, be you, and be honest about your journey. That's what people will connect with.

Another thing, don't just talk to people. Talk with them. Engagement is the magic word on the internet. Reply to comments, thank people for sharing and get into conversations. It's like being at a party and mingling, except you do it from your phone or computer.

And you know what? The more you share, the more you'll find your community—people who dig what you do and want to support you. It's cool to start seeing the same names popping up in your notifications, cheering you on. That's when you know you're starting to build your tribe.

It would help if you also were a bit of a detective. Use the tools out there to see what works and what doesn't. Most platforms have some analytics, a fancy way of saying, "checking out how well your stuff is doing." See what people like the most, and do more of that. It's like getting instant feedback on your performance.

Remember, though, the internet's a big place, and it's easy to get lost in the crowd. It might take a while before you get noticed. That's okay. Every big name started as just another person trying to get their voice heard. Keep at it, keep sharing, and keep honing your skills.

Using the internet to tell the world about your awesome skill is about connecting. It's about building bridges between you and people who are into the same things you are. It's about creating a space where your skill can shine and you can find others who shine just like you. So, go ahead, grab that digital megaphone, and start showing the world what you've got. Who knows where it might lead?

CHAPTER 15

LEAVING FOOTPRINTS YOUR SKILL'S LEGACY

Imagine you've got this cool thing you're good at. You're awesome at cooking, playing guitar, coding, or gardening. Now, think about everyone around you, in your town or worldwide. Every time you share your cooking, play a tune, fix a bug in a program, or plant a beautiful garden, you're putting a little piece of yourself out there.

Your skill isn't just about you getting better at something. It's about touching people's lives. Maybe someone eats your food and thinks, "That's the best thing I've ever tasted." Maybe someone hears you play guitar, which makes them want to learn, too. Or you could code a website, and it helps someone find the information they need or brings a smile to their face with its cool design. Or your garden gives people a place to sit and feel peaceful.

Whenever you do something with your skill, you toss a pebble into a big lake. The ripples from that pebble spread out far. Even when the pebble sinks, and you can't see it anymore, the ripples keep going. That's like your skill. Even when you're not around, the things you did — the meals, the music, the websites, the gardens — keep having an effect. They keep making waves.

That's how you leave a mark on the world. It's not just about being famous or making tons of money. It's about those ripples. It's about making someone's day brighter, inspiring someone to try something new, or just adding a bit of beauty to the world. That's the kind of dream to have — that long after you're gone, the ripples from your skill keep spreading, keep making the world a better place, bit by bit.

Be inspired by stories of people who've made a difference with their skills

First up, there's this person named Ben. Ben was one of those tech experts who could figure out anything to do with PCs. He experienced childhood in a humble community where only a few had a lot of familiarity with innovation. Ben might have gone to a significant city and made boatloads of money. However, he had another thought. He began free coding studios for youngsters in his town. At the end of the week, the nearby public venue was loaded with kids tapping away at consoles and building their sites and games. Ben instructed them that they could get wizardry going on screen with a couple of lines of code. Years later, some of these children began their tech organizations, and they generally remembered where they started.

Then there's Maria. Maria was about gardens. She could make anything blossom anywhere. In any case, she didn't remain quiet about this ability. She began a local garden project in a city where Dark had dominated. She showed every individual who joined—from young children to old granddads—how to focus on plants. This nursery turned into a desert garden, a little green heaven where individuals came to plant, meet neighbors, and inhale a piece more straightforwardly. That nursery is still there; presently, there are more similar ones, transforming void parts into patches of green.

Presently, we should discuss Jamal. He had a voice that could make you stop anything that you were doing and tune in. He cherished music, and he utilized his ability to unite individuals. He coordinated shows where the music was an exciting treat. He joined artists from everywhere, blending classes and styles, showing that music has no limits. Jamal's shows fund-raised for many good purposes, from building schools to giving clean water. Moreover, he didn't simply sing — he conversed with individuals, shared stories, and spread a message of solidarity and trust.

Also, shouldn't something be said about Anna? She had a talent for cooking. Her hands could prepare dishes that were a gala for the faculties. Be that as it may, she didn't turn into a gourmet specialist in some perfect quality eatery. Anna began a program where she cooked with individuals going through difficult stretches — the needy people recuperating from disease or required organization. Her kitchen was a position of warmth and giggling, and her dinners with these people gave something beyond sustenance; they gave a feeling of family.

There's additionally this teen, Tony. Tony cherished skating. He was great at it, as well. However, in his city, there wasn't required to have been a protected spot to skate. Rather than simply wishing things were unique, Tony got going. He talked at local gatherings, assembled help, and assisted in planning a skate with stopping. Presently, there's where anybody with a board can come and skate without stress. Tony didn't stop there. He tutors more youthful skaters, showing them stunts and about security and regard for other people.

These accounts have an ongoing idea — an individual intensely and an expertise who looks past themselves. However, they consider their expertise a device for individual increase but for building something more significant. They comprehend that what they're great at can give pleasure, instruct, unite individuals, and recuperate.

Ben, Maria, Jamal, Anna, and Tony may be in just some set of experiences books or have films made about them. Be that as it may, they've had a genuine effect on their sides of the world. The waves they've made with their abilities continue spreading, contacting lives in ways they probably won't be aware of.

These are the sorts of stories that make you ponder what you're great at. You might be perfect at composing, playing soccer, fixing vehicles, or drawing. You could make the best chocolate chip treats around or be great at paying attention to individuals. Whatever it is, contemplate how you can utilize it to accomplish something great. It doesn't need to be a colossal thing. Start little, in your way, locally.

Each expert can have an effect. Everything revolves around how you use it. Improving things is tied to seeing the potential, even in the littlest ways. Your ability could be the way to open up your actual capacity and the capability of others.

So, what's your expertise? What's more, how can you make waves in the lake? Motivate others while likewise being motivated by utilizing these accounts. At last, it's something beyond being known for what you can do. It's tied in with being associated with what you've offered in return. What's more, that is an inheritance worth leaving.

We began by looking at how to gain some new practical knowledge. Everything revolves around making those first strides and staying with it, in any event, when it's hard.

Remember, it's not just about being great immediately; it's tied in with getting better each time you attempt.

We discussed finding a guide who knows a ton and can help you en route. This individual resembles a mentor who's been there previously and can give you the general tour.

Getting criticism on the thing you're doing is significant, as well. It resembles having somebody let you know what's working and what's not so you can continue to improve. What's more, having the option to change your arrangements when things don't go right is no joking matter. It assists you with continuing to push ahead, come what may.

We've shared tales about individuals who don't surrender and continue to buckle down until they arrive at their objectives. Furthermore, we looked at how to take what you're great at and make it something you can bring in cash from. It's tied in with transforming your expertise into something meaningful for others.

Then, at that point, the part about spreading the word about your name for your specialization. It's tied in with telling individuals you're great at something so they come to you when required.

We've likewise examined utilizing the Web to let everybody know what you can do. It is something else that you can impart your stuff to the world with only a couple of snaps.

At last, we contemplated how you can imprint on the world with your abilities. Like establishing a tree, it continues to develop even after you're gone.

What's going on to detract from this? Keep at it. Learn and get better consistently. Help other people, and let them help you. Make your abilities sparkle and offer them to the world. Furthermore, recall that what you're doing today can be something individuals remember for quite a while.

This isn't simply the end of a book; it's the perfect start for you. It's your story now, and you have all you want to make it incredible. Continue and accomplish something astonishing with what you've realized!

www.ingramcontent.com/pod-product-compliance
Lightning Source LLC
Chambersburg PA
CBHW070448050426
42451CB00015B/3391